Better Homes and Gardens®

TILING

TILING IDEAS AND TECHNIQUES
FOR YOUR HOME

Meredith® Books
Des Moines, Iowa

Better Homes and Gardens® Tiling
Editor: Larry Johnston
Copy Chief: Terri Fredrickson
Publishing Operations Manager: Karen Schirm
Senior Editor, Asset and Information Manager: Phillip Morgan
Edit and Design Production Coordinator: Mary Lee Gavin
Editorial and Design Assistant: Renee E. McAtee
Book Production Managers: Pam Kvitne,
    Marjorie J. Schenkelberg, Rick von Holdt, Mark Weaver
Contributing Copy Editor: Steve Hallam
Contributing Proofreaders: Tom Blackett, Monica Bruno,
    Cheri Madison
Contributing Editorial Assistant: Janet Anderson
Indexer: Barbara L. Klein

**Additional Editorial Contributions from
    Abramowitz Design**
Publishing Director/Designer: Tim Abramowitz
Writer: Martin Miller
Designer: Joel Wires
Photo Researcher: Amber Jones
Photography: Image Studios
    Account Executive: Lisa Egan
    Photographers: Glen Hartjes, Will Croff, John von Dorn
    Assistants: Bill Kapinski
    Stylist: Karla Kaphaem
    Technical Advisor: Rick Nadke
Additional Photography: Doug Hetherington
Illustration: Art Rep Services, Inc.
    Director: Chip Nadeau
    Illustrator: Dave Brandon

Meredith® Books
Executive Director, Editorial: Gregory H. Kayko
Executive Director, Design: Matt Strelecki
Executive Editor/Group Manager: Larry Erickson
Senior Associate Design Director: Tom Wegner
Marketing Product Manager: Isaac Petersen

Publisher and Editor in Chief: James D. Blume
Editorial Director: Linda Raglan Cunningham
Executive Director, New Business Development: Todd M. Davis
Executive Director, Sales: Ken Zagor
Director, Operations: George A. Susral
Director, Production: Douglas M. Johnston
Director, Marketing: Amy Nichols
Business Director: Jim Leonard

Vice President and General Manager: Douglas J. Guendel

Meredith Publishing Group
President: Jack Griffin
Executive Vice President: Bob Mate

Meredith Corporation
Chairman and Chief Executive Officer: William T. Kerr
President and Chief Operating Officer: Stephen M. Lacy

In Memoriam: E. T. Meredith III (1933-2003)

All of us at Meredith® Books are dedicated to
providing you with the information and ideas you
need to enhance your home and garden. We welcome
your comments and suggestions. Write to us at:
Meredith Books
Home Improvement Books Department
1716 Locust St.
Des Moines, IA 50309–3023

If you would like to purchase any of our home
improvement, gardening, cooking, crafts, or home
decorating and design books, check wherever quality
books are sold. Or visit us at: bhgbooks.com

Note to the Readers: Due to differing conditions,
tools, and individual skills, Meredith Corporation
assumes no responsibility for any damages, injuries
suffered, or losses incurred as a result of following the
information published in this book. Before beginning
any project, review the instructions carefully, and if
any doubts or questions remain, consult local experts
or authorities. Because codes and regulations vary
greatly, you always should check with authorities to
ensure that your project complies with all applicable
local codes and regulations. Always read and observe
all of the safety precautions provided by
manufacturers of any tools, equipment, or supplies,
and follow all accepted safety procedures.

TABLE OF CONTENTS

CHAPTER HIGHLIGHTS

This chapter discusses the kinds of tile

available to today's do-it-yourself

homeowner and includes tips and

techniques for laying out and

installing them. You'll also find hints

that will help you select the right tile

for any room in the house.

DESIGNING WITH TILE

Some things about tile just don't change. When you're shopping for tile, you'll find ceramic and stone products that have been around for centuries, materials that can hardly be improved upon. But you'll also find tile made of new materials that are constantly undergoing improvement. New vinyls are tough and finished with coatings that need almost no care. If you see some of them from the next room, you might mistake them for stone, wood, or ceramic tile. You can snap together a laminate floor in the dining room in an afternoon, then move the dining table back for an evening dinner party.

And cork is making a comeback, now finished with stain-resistant coatings. New carpet tiles are softer, tougher, and easier to maintain than older varieties. Ceramic tile, the longtime standard of style and elegance, used to require expensive professional installation. But it's a major do-it-yourself material now that easy-to-use thinset mortars and organic mastics are available. In short, there's a huge variety of high-quality tiling materials from which you can choose. One or perhaps more will be perfectly suited to your standards, your budget, and your room.

TILE FOR EVERY ROOM

Tile was once assumed to be a material best used in the kitchen, bathroom, and perhaps the entryway of a home.

Tile is more versatile today. You can use almost any tile in any room including dining rooms, family rooms, and children's rooms. What kind of tile you choose depends on a combination of factors, including your budget, how you will use the room, and whether style or practicality is of greater importance.

Tile is available in countless styles, materials, and colors, so finding the right tile for any location will probably not be difficult. The choice will be easier if you focus your attention on considerations of durability and design. Many manufacturers offer help in answering the question, "What tile should I use for my particular project?" Suggested uses for each type of tile are often listed on the carton. These guidelines are based on standards of durability and maintenance. Remember that you are the best judge of style and design ideas for your home.

Design, first and foremost, is simplicity—a unified mood or look that is both visually appealing and physically comfortable. Design begins with decisions not about aesthetics, but about how you want to use a room. After that, you can

▲ Vinyl tile is ideal for kitchens. Available in a wide variety of colors and patterns to match any kitchen style, vinyl tile is easy to install and to maintain.

▼ Ceramic tile is a traditional flooring for kitchens. The hard surface resists scuffing and is easy to keep clean.

◀ Neutral-color ceramic tile makes an elegant floor in this dining room. The unobtrusive color and design highlight the furnishings.

use any kind of tile that complements that use as well as the preferences of your personality.

A family room that's the center of much activity, for example, may call for a bold, bright tile design. In a formal dining or living room, you may want the tile to blend with—and almost recede into—the surroundings.

Style can be broadly categorized as either formal or informal. Within those categories are variations based on architecture, geography, and historical period. Don't be overly concerned with terms or formulas—they may cause you to choose a style you're not comfortable with.

Formal installations are characterized by regular geometric shapes and symmetrical arrangements. Even so, they can still look lively and exciting. Informal designs may incorporate curves, asymmetrical elements, and random colors or shapes.

Period designs can be personalized by incorporating neutral-colored tiles as a contrast to the often dark tones of the Arts-and-Crafts

style, for instance, or by adding linear borders around the curves of a Mediterranean pattern. A contemporary design scheme may include many formal elements but can be softened with curved outlines and irregular contours.

Your own intuition is your best guide to room style. Trends in interior design, especially for floors, now tend to favor muted or neutral colors, but you can create a room with bold character and individuality if that's your style.

▼ Tile is a natural on bathroom floors and walls, where resistance to moisture is a must. Ceramic tile offers style and durability.

KITCHENS

Tile seems right at home in the kitchen. That's because a kitchen has lots of surfaces ideally suited to various kinds of tile—the floor, walls, countertops, an island, and backsplashes. These surfaces are the primary design elements in a kitchen, along with the appliances and furniture.

Plan your floor first. When you've chosen your floor tile, you've set the style for probably half of the total design space, which helps set the tone for the rest.

First decide if you want the floor to serve as a background for the rest of the features in the room or as a prominent design element. Choose a neutral color for a floor that won't overpower other elements. You can create a subtle interest by varying textures and patterns on the floor. For example, alternating earth tones with cream-colored tiles will keep the floor from looking uniform and dull. Yet this scheme will still create a surface that blends with most cabinets and countertops. Porcelain tiles and tumbled marble also create the same effect with a natural, rough-hewn, or Mediterranean texture.

▼ **This kitchen features black and white vinyl tiles in a diagonal checkerboard pattern that makes a bold floor with a traditional look. The floor is one of the first things you notice in this kitchen.**

▼ **A tiled wall between the countertop and the bottom of the cabinets replaces a low backsplash in this kitchen.**

If you want a more dramatic floor, increase the intensity of the color scheme, add borders, or insert accent tiles at regular or random intervals throughout the design.

Countertop design is no longer limited to a standard preformed laminate work surface with a short integral backsplash. A 4-inch backsplash isn't necessarily a thing of the past, but many new kitchen designs include taller backsplashes or tile covering the entire wall behind a countertop. A backsplash or wall with hand-painted tiles, geometric patterns, or a mural provides both a functional and artistic backdrop for the counter.

▶ Neutral-color textured tiles fit the look of this old-country kitchen. Glazed green tiles behind and beside the range highlight the cooking area with a splash of color.

You can treat the walls as an extension of the design theme of other surfaces or as a separate element that blends with the others. Like floors, walls tend to be a backdrop for the rest of the room, so their colors are normally muted and neutral. But you can create strategic accents, especially on a large expanse, with colorful tiled panels. Tile can add texture to walls too.

Appearance is important, but kitchen tile should also be tough and durable. Ceramic tile and stone are common choices for floors, walls, and countertops. If you're concerned about dishes and cookware breaking on the hard surface, add area rugs. Radiant heating under the tile can keep the floor and the room at comfortable temperatures throughout. Parquet brings rich, warm wood tones and a subtle patterned texture to a kitchen floor. Properly sealed and maintained, parquet will last in a kitchen for years.

Resilients and laminates resist the rigors of a kitchen floor well, and provide plenty of design options at a reduced cost. Carpet tile is the least practical tile for a kitchen floor. It's warm and soft, but stains easily.

FINDING THE RIGHT DESIGN

Making decisions about home design and decoration starts with gathering ideas. First, make some notes about what you like and dislike in your home and other homes you've been in. Put the notes in a folder along with anything you can clip out of interior design magazines. Don't forget your newspaper—many newspaper weekend editions carry well-informed articles on home design.

Go shopping at your home center and independent retailers. Include the large tile chains too. Get samples wherever you can and lay them out on your floor and countertop. Tape them to the walls. Get more ideas on the Internet.

As you work through this process, you'll find you are drawn to certain styles, themes, color combinations, and patterns. These will form a style, almost without your knowing it. Keep these ideas in mind as you develop a design scheme.

BATHROOMS

Because bathrooms usually have tile on floors and shower walls, your first thought in planning to tile a bathroom might be to treat each as a separate surface.

But most bathrooms look best with a unified tile design, grouping the tub surround, vanity, walls, and floor together as an ensemble. An easy way to unify your theme is to use similar-size tile and vary the color from surface to surface.

▼ Different tile sizes and shapes bring style and variety to this bathroom, even if the colors are about the same.

Resilient and laminate tile (with glued joints to seal out the water) provide an economical, long-lasting bathroom floor option. Carpet tile, parquet, and cork are not recommended for master or family baths because water might damage them. You might want to use them, however, in a half bath or guest bath, where they won't be subject to constant water splashes or a parade of wet feet. Ceramic and stone tile are the most durable (and most costly) choices. They also offer you the most design choices. Install electric radiant floor mats before you lay the tile for greater comfort.

If you're using resilient tile or laminate tile on the floor, available sizes and shapes will be limited, but if you're using an ensemble theme, you can tile the walls and vanity with a ceramic or stone tile that complements the color of the floor.

Overall, smaller ceramic tiles—4 inches or smaller—offer the most flexibility. Smaller tiles are easier to fit around vanities, tubs, and fixtures. Small tiles are easier to cut and trim. For example, it's easier to fit 3½- or 4-inch tiles around the curved corners of a tub than 8-inch ones.

Use vitreous tile for floors—unglazed to prevent slipping. Glazed tiles work well on walls and vanity tops. You can use matte-finished tiles anywhere, of course, but they are harder to clean. Sealing them will make cleaning a little

▶ Tile fits well into contemporary room styles. Curves and colors enliven this design, which would otherwise be formal, with straight lines and square corners.

easier and will help protect them from mildew growth. Mosaic tiles are also great for making safe (and stylish) floors. Their close, grouted joints create a virtually slip-free surface.

A small room like a bathroom can take on a new look with some horizontal lines. Walls are best suited to this technique. A ceramic cap along the top of tiled wainscoting, for example, will make the room seem larger. So will a border along the edges of a tiled floor or a

contrasting tile line on the length of the vanity. Ceramic tile or stone on the vanity countertop and backsplash also creates a surface that's attractive and easy to clean.

The hard surface of ceramic and stone tile—even a large laminate floor—can alter the acoustics of a room. To keep the sound from bouncing around a hard-surfaced room, put all your fluffiest towels on towel bars or open shelving.

▲ Painted tiles frame the mirror and window in this bathroom. Other decorative tiles adorn the front of the vanity and some are randomly placed in the shower walls. Such accents give this bathroom an informal look.

▼ Yellow and white floor tiles make a high-key floor in this bright bathroom.

FAMILY SPACES

▲ Large stone or stone-look floor tiles lend an informal air to a room. The floor style in this living room complements the comfortable and casual furniture.

that kitchen floors do, and they can be formal or quite casual, depending on your taste.

Parquet tile will create a traditional, formal atmosphere, but so will laminate tile in a wood pattern. Even vinyl tile in muted tones or a grid pattern can look formal. Install tile with a floral or geometric pattern, and the floor will fit more informal themes. Or, use dark cork tile or carpet tile with its pile direction set to make it look like a broadloom weave. Carpet will be more difficult to keep clean, however.

Family rooms are in constant use, with heavy traffic, but their atmosphere is informal. Choose a high-quality, dense floor tile, such as large porcelain pavers or slate, that can take the abuse and not show wear. Irregularly shaped tiles add a touch of informality. Laminate tiles and resilients also stand up to family-room use, and their lower price and abundance of styles allow you to have a durable floor without sacrificing aesthetics.

Tile for family spaces has to fulfill both practical and aesthetic demands. Making these choices will be easier if you think less about the style of the room and more about how you will use the space.

Rather than thinking of your dining room as a room with a particular style, for instance, think of it simply as a room where people eat. That takes the emphasis off conventional thinking and may spur your creativity. Dining room floors don't have to endure the hard use

Children's rooms are also perfect for laminates and resilients, spaces where low maintenance, low cost, and informality are important considerations. Carpet tile is also a good choice for a child's room, especially for younger children. Carpet texture will soften falls

◀ Textured stone gives a rugged, ancient look to this library and sitting room. Area rugs serve as accents and help section off parts of the room.

and reduce noise, and if you can't remove crayon marks or spilled finger paints, you can easily pry up the damaged section and replace it.

Family spaces are usually the largest rooms in the house, so they'll present you with a large area to use pattern and texture as design elements. The rough and often uneven texture of brick tile or handmade pavers will impart a rustic and relaxed mood to a floor pattern. More uniform machine-made tiles are more formal. On walls, vary the texture by mingling embossed tiles with glazed tiles.

Consider the size of the tile in relation to the floor size when planning your

floor layout. The combination of scale and texture can dramatically alter the appearance of a room. Large tiles call attention to themselves and can make a room seem smaller. Small tiles, on the other hand, can look lost in a large room.

HIDING TAPERED TILES

An out-of-square floor means you'll have tapered tiles on at least one edge. Hide tapered tiles under cabinetry or behind furniture (left). Also, a diagonal layout (right) or larger, irregular tiles can minimize the effects of a tapered edge.

SPECIAL INSTALLATIONS

Ceramic tile is often used for floors, walls, and countertops. But you can install ceramic tile in far more places than just these standard surfaces. Ceramic tiles are perfect for stair risers, fireplaces, mantels, hearths, fountains, baseboards, floor accents, window borders, crown molding, and more features. Installing tile on many of these surfaces calls for specific techniques and materials.

When tiling a fireplace or stove surround, for example, use a heat-resistant thinset or epoxy mortar. You can tile over existing fireplace brick or stone that's in good condition, but you'll have to level the surface with mortar. Screed the mortar from the floor to the underside of the mantel using a 2×4 to make this job easy. If the tile layout requires you to cut narrow tiles along the edges, consider replacing the edge tiles with border tiles. Borders look better than narrow field tiles.

Tiled stair risers can transform the appearance

▼ Tile makes the fireplace and hearth stand out in this room. Using the same color for the tile and painted trim ties the room elements together.

▼ Tile works well with wood-burning stoves, protecting the floor and walls from sparks and embers.

of an interior stairway because of the contrast between the tile color and texture and the wood tread. Most floor tiles are too thick—with mortar, they'll stick out past the tread nosing. Instead, use standard wall tiles or stone. Set the tile on ¼-inch backerboard if there is room under the nosing.

Window recesses take on added architectural interest when clad in ceramic tile. You can tile only the recess or combine the tiled recess with a tiled window surround on the wall. If tiling the recess and surround, or if the window is in a wall that is tiled completely, as it might be in a kitchen or bathroom, use bullnose tiles or corner

◀ Tile on the wall continues into the arched window recess for an unexpected architectural element in this kitchen.

▼ Tile on the floor brings style to this basement recreation room. Random colors give the linear layout a crisp, contemporary look.

edging tiles where the wall and recess meet.

Foyers and entryways can present problems if the floor area is small. Out-of-square walls will require taper-cut edge tiles, and most foyers don't have furniture you can use to hide them. A diagonal tile layout can solve the problem because the pattern itself becomes the most visible element, and the crooked walls are less noticeable without straight edges as references. Consider a geometric pattern; foyers are a good place to show off an interesting tile layout, which will downplay narrow edges. Create a design that takes up one-fourth to one-half of the floor space so the floor will look balanced.

Special installations like these are just right for achieving some really decorative effects with a combination of field tiles and handmade accent tiles. Ask your tile dealer about accent tiles or search the Internet for "handmade tiles."

THE STYLE OF TILE

When you design a tile installation, especially one for a large surface, look at the entire room or area as a unit. That way, you'll be able to integrate the design into the overall theme of the room, and any purely decorative aspect won't look like an afterthought.

To integrate decorative tiles into a layout, start by looking at tiles that match the colors and sizes of the regular tiles. Some manufacturers make decorative borders for their regular lines. A few handmade decorative tiles used as accents can be sized differently than the rest of the field tiles, but mix sizes carefully. If you order custom tiles from an artist or craftsperson, be sure to provide a sketch that includes the colors and tile dimensions.

Decorative tiles are expensive and can quickly put your installation over budget, so avoid using too many of these tiles. And a few hand-painted, relief, or tumbled-marble tiles spread throughout the installation will be more effective than a large number of them. Every accent calls attention to itself, and more than a few can look chaotic. If patterned border tiles stretch your budget too far, try regular field tiles of a different color for a border.

Color is the most powerful design element in any installation. That's because we see color first, before texture or pattern, and because colors evoke emotions; there's a reason that a melancholy mood is described as "blue."

The effect of color on the mood or feel of a room is subtle, so describing it is complicated. Here are some standard color moods:

▼ Colorful random tiles harmonize with the colors and pattern of the wallpaper in this bathroom.

▼ A border of decorative tiles highlights this vanity. The border colors complement the vanity tiles and the basin.

▶ Painted tiles create a mural on this kitchen wall. While the effect is striking, you have to be sure your fondness for it will last. Changing tiled wall decor will be much more difficult than repainting or hanging new wallpaper.

■ Reds and oranges suggest excitement; darker shades create warmth.

■ Yellows and whites seem cheery and can brighten a dark room. Too much of them, however, can be overpowering or sterile.

■ Greens and blues create calm; deep tones suggest wealth, strength, and status.

■ Black makes large rooms seem smaller. It is also an excellent accent and can suggest elegance or urbanity.

The value of a color—how bright or how dark it is—can also affect the design. Low values (deep burgundy, for example) recede and can make a room seem smaller. High values (bright green, for example) stand out and can make a room seem large and airy.

The colors in a tile installation work together to create a surface that either dominates a room or acts as a backdrop. A pattern with high contrasts (a checkerboard of white and black tile, for example) calls attention to itself and away from other elements in the room. Pastel tiles or tiles with earth tones are less showy and allow other features of the room to stand out.

USE COLOR CAREFULLY

Color is the most powerful design element, so you should use it with care. These guidelines can help make your color selection easier:

■ Trust your impulses. You have certain conscious and subliminal color preferences, and letting them express your style will result in a design that pleases you.

■ Ignore commercial color names. Designations such as "Autumn gold" or "Georgian blue" are purposely loaded with emotional adjectives. These fanciful names can lead you in the wrong direction.

■ Take color samples home. Get more than one tile of each color if you can—colors can look different as they take up more space. Samples look different at home than they do in the store—largely a result of differences in lighting. To see what they'll really look like in your home, set the sample tiles on the floor or countertop, or tape them to the wall. Then look at them at different times of the day.

TILING THE GREAT OUTDOORS

There are fewer material options for outdoor tile projects than for indoor tiling. Only ceramic, cement-bodied, and stone tile are rated for outdoor installation. Also, the tile must be laid over a concrete slab or other surface that will withstand weather.

Ceramic tile is an ideal material for outdoor projects. So are some, but not all, stone varieties. The first priority when planning an outdoor tile project is to match your tile choice to your climate.

Saltillo and other soft-bodied tiles are fine for warm climates, but they'll absorb water and crack in harsh winter freezes. So will many stone tiles—including some granites. Freezing climates call for hard-bodied tiles, such as porcelain, which won't crack when the temperature plunges.

No matter what tile you choose, it should have a nonslip surface. Ask your dealer to recommend tiles you can use outdoors and that won't get slippery when they're wet.

Like indoor projects, outdoor installations require a solid foundation; on patios, that means a 3- or 4-inch concrete slab. In many localities,

pouring a slab will require a building permit and perhaps inspections by the local building department. Before you start, ask the building department about codes regulating the thickness of a slab, the kind of reinforcement it should have, and whether you need a permit.

Projects with roofs or walls—a covered patio or outdoor kitchen with a perimeter wall, for example—will probably need footings: thicker, reinforced sections of concrete made to support heavy loads. Even if you don't plan to add a roof until sometime in the future, pour the

▲ If you're tiling a swimming-pool deck, wait until the pool is installed before starting the slab. The depth of the excavation should put the deck tile flush with the top of the pool.

▲ Saltillo is a handmade, soft-bodied tile that will readily absorb water. It—along with other handmade tile—is the preferred tile for warm climates and Southwest designs, but will crack in freezing climates.

◀ Ceramic tile makes a patio that's durable and easy to maintain, a great place to relax or entertain family and friends.

footing when you pour the slab. You'll save a considerable amount of time and money later.

Pouring a new slab has an advantage you don't have when tiling in existing rooms—you can design the slab with dimensions that will fit some multiple of your tile size. That way, your tile installation will be the same size as the slab, and you won't have to cut tiles for the edges. Even so, you may have to adjust tile spacing to get the layout to fit perfectly, because pouring a slab to the precise size needed is not easy.

Another difference between outdoor and indoor installations is scale. You can usually lay larger tiles—up to 2 feet square—for a patio because you have more room to work with and the area isn't surrounded by walls that limit proportions. You can cover an area with large tiles faster than with small ones, but there are drawbacks. Large tiles don't lend themselves to

as much design flexibility as a 9- or 12-inch tile, for example, and they often require more cutting. Their weight makes them harder to line up too.

▲ Flagstones can be bluestone, limestone, redstone, sandstone, granite, or slate. The irregular shapes of flagstones are suitable for both casual and formal designs. Cut stone is cut to size with straight edges and square corners.

MATERIALS

As you consider which tile to use, you'll become familiar with these material options:

■ **Carpet tile** is the least costly tile and one of the easiest to install. It is also the most limited in its applications. You could put it in a little-used guest bath, but it's generally not suited to wet locations or rooms receiving heavy traffic. It is, however, the softest underfoot and can bring comfort to bedroom floors, especially those in children's rooms.

■ **Ceramic tile** is the most durable tile, making it an excellent choice for floors, countertops, and walls in almost any room or for any outdoor installation. It's durable because it's hard, so it is uncomfortable to stand on for long periods and can shatter dropped plates and glasses. These concerns often can be reduced with area rugs or cushions. Ceramic tile comes in a vast array of colors, shapes, and sizes.

■ **Vinyl,** originally developed to meet the need for inexpensive flooring with the look of stone or ceramic tile, has matured since those early days. It's sometimes hard to tell at a glance now whether you're looking at a top-of-the-line vinyl or real stone or ceramic tile. This tile has more soundproofing ability than its thinness would seem to indicate. It's a good floor material for families with young children—it's soft underfoot, less likely than ceramics to break dishes or cause bruises, and it cleans up quickly. Maintenance usually amounts to no more than regular damp-mopping.

■ **Laminate tile** has been popular in Europe for more than half a century. Thanks to the miracles of photo technology and the chemistry of plastics, laminate tiles are reasonably priced imitations of stone, wood, and ceramic materials. Melamine, one of the toughest plastics, gives the tile its durability. Mass production and inexpensive base materials keep prices low; laminates are usually less costly than ceramic tile, but more expensive than vinyl. Laminates are usually easy for do-it-yourselfers to install.

■ **Parquet** is a special class of tile: It's made from thin strips of wood. When installed with a mastic adhesive, it looks like an inlaid wood floor, with all the warm wood tones that can't be duplicated by any synthetic product. Parquet tiles are suitable only for dry locations, and have traditionally been installed on dining room floors, a perfect use for their inherent formality. It's also a good choice for

▼ **Light-color tile brings a fresh look to this dining room. It's also easy to clean if young diners have a spill.**

a formal sitting room, den, office, or library. Parquet can be used with stone or ceramic tile for an elegant entry hall.

- **Cork** brings to a room the color and texture of a natural material. Cork, which comes from tree bark, is porous, which makes it springy, comfortable, warm, and sound-deadening. Different shades of its warm brown color are achieved by heating it. It comes coated with a polyurethane varnish, but will stain.

- **Stone tile** has been used in homes since the earliest times. Such an age-old natural product can hardly be described as having gotten better over time, but more varieties are available now. Marble, granite, and slate are traditional favorites. Limestone and quartzite are newer options.

  - **Granite** is the hardest and most durable stone tile. Its grays, greens, reds, blacks, and browns give it a wide design latitude that fits contemporary and traditional design themes. It's less porous than marble and sandstones so it resists stains better, but it still requires sealing.

  - **Marble** for tile occurs in soft greens, grays, pinks, blues, and yellows, as well as shades of black and white. Marble is porous, which makes it prone to staining, even when sealed. It wears more quickly than granite, but the wear adds to its charm.

  - **Slate** comes polished or with ridges. Its colors range from shades of black and gray

to purples, reds, and greens. This dense stone resists stains, and you can wax it for a higher sheen.

- **Limestone** is a hard rock with a soft appearance, developing a smooth texture as it's used. Its colors are neutral—pale grays and yellows—so it makes a good background where you want your furnishings to be the focal point. It needs sealing to keep it from staining.

- **Quartzite** is hard and dense, and it comes in a variety of neutral colors.

A QUICK GUIDE TO TILE

Most tiles are well-suited to use throughout the house. Here's a quick glance at their versatility.

Resilients (vinyl)—Use in playrooms, family rooms, bathrooms, kitchens, or anywhere durability and affordability matter. Not suitable for outdoor installations, but can be used below grade (in a basement).

Parquet—Use in living rooms, dining rooms, kitchens (if properly sealed), or any other room in which durability and style are priorities. Cannot be used below grade, in baths, or outdoors.

Laminate—Use in any room in which durability is required at an affordable cost. Can be used in rooms below grade with proper joint sealing; otherwise susceptible to water damage. Not for use outdoors.

Cork—Use in any room that requires a unique floor style, where sound insulation is preferred. Not for baths, rooms below grade, or the outdoors.

Carpet—Use in any dry room in which comfort and low cost are important. Not generally suitable for use in kitchens or baths, below grade, or outdoors.

Ceramic and stone—Use in kitchens, bathrooms, family rooms, or almost any other room where durability and design are priorities. Good for countertops and walls. Can be installed below grade and outdoors.

CERAMIC AND CEMENT-BODIED TILE

▼ Of all the ceramic tiles, porcelain is gaining most in popularity. It absorbs virtually no moisture, comes glazed or unglazed in a variety of sizes, and has many stone-like textures.

Ceramic tile is made from refined clays that have been extruded or pressed into a mold, then fired (baked) one or more times at high temperature. In the marketplace, the term "ceramic tile" is loosely applied to all kinds of tiles, including some that are not technically ceramics. You'll find terra-cotta, saltillo, and other handmade tiles lumped together with porcelain and quarry tiles and other true ceramics. What is common to all of these tiles is that they provide a hard, durable surface for floors, walls, and countertops. Also, they are available in more colors, patterns, and textures than any other kind of tile.

Tile is rated as impervious, vitreous, semivitreous, or nonvitreous, depending on how porous, or water-absorbent, it is. Impervious and vitreous tiles are least absorbent, so they're best for tub and shower surrounds and floors that will get wet, including a patio. Semivitreous tile is good for floors in dry places, and nonvitreous tile is suitable for walls.

■ *Ceramic tile* comes glazed or unglazed. Glazes add both color and protection.

Glazed tiles are water-resistant, but can be dangerously slick when wet. They're not for floors, but can really make a countertop or wall installation sparkle. Tile with slip-resistant glaze is available. You don't need to seal glazed tiles, but you should seal the grout joints to make them water-resistant and to keep them from staining.

Unglazed tiles have a softer, less light-reflective surface, which makes them a good choice for informal country or rustic looks.

■ *Cement-bodied tile* is made from a molded and cured sand-and-mortar mix. A nonvitreous tile, it is the other popular standard of the tile family. Some are cast in

▲ Quarry tiles can be either semivitreous or vitreous. They come in ½- to ¾-inch thicknesses and in a variety of shapes: 4- to 12-inch squares and hexagons, and 3×6-inch or 4×8-inch rectangles.

rough textures that mimic cleft stone—at a fraction of the cost of the natural material. Cement-bodied tiles are a less expensive, long-lasting imitation of ceramics that works well in many applications.

Some tiles are made for specific purposes:

■ *Pavers,* at least ½ inch thick and machine made or handmade, are designed primarily for floors. Vitreous pavers can be used as wall or countertop tiles.

■ *Brick veneer* will work in both outdoor and indoor locations, both wet and dry. Its rough texture, however, will prove almost impossible to clean in shower surrounds.

■ *Wall tiles,* usually ¼ inch thick in 4¼- and 6-inch squares, are softer than floor tiles and nonvitreous, so they are unsuited to other uses.

Ceramic tile is made and marketed as either *loose tiles,* individual tiles that you set separately,

▼ Terra-cotta tile is suitable for dry areas. It comes sealed or unsealed in 3- to 12-inch squares and in other geometric shapes.

▼ Cement-bodied tiles come with both rough and smooth finishes, in 6- to 9-inch squares or rectangles and in large mesh-backed paver sheets of up to 36 inches.

or *sheet-mounted tiles,* which are glued to a mesh backing and set as a unit. The individual tiles on a sheet are usually 4 inches wide or less and are prespaced, which reduces installation time. Mosaic tiles are sheet-mounted tiles that are 2 inches wide or less.

Ceramic and cement-bodied tiles can be applied with several kinds of adhesive and on several substrates. The most durable installation is in thinset over cement backerboard.

▼ Saltillo tile is the perfect choice in rustic and Southwestern designs and comes in a variety of shapes and sizes.

TRIM TILE

Trim tile has two purposes—it gives a finished appearance to the corners of a tile installation and it hides the square, unglazed edges (or cut edges) of field tiles. In these ways, trim tiles soften the appearance of a tiled surface.

Most regular trim tile creates rounded edges and is made in a variety of shapes, each one designed to cover a specific application. Regular trim is fired in the same pattern and with the same color or glaze as the field tile—only its shape is different than the adjacent tiles.

Border tile is a type of trim tile with a shape, color, or design made to outline the edges of a tiled surface, to accent it, or to separate different sections of field tile. A border sets off the field tiles from the rest of the tiles on a floor, wall, or countertop. Many border styles come as mosaic patterns—prespaced in narrow sheets and mounted on a mesh backing.

Trim tile falls into two categories. You'll need *surface trim* when the tile surface is on the same plane as the surrounding surface, as when the tile is inset into a surface. Use *radius trim* when the tile is higher than the surrounding surface.

Here are some kinds of trim tile you can use to finish various edges:

- *Aprons* are half tiles rounded on one edge and made to fill narrow surfaces, such as the front of a countertop.

- *Bases* define the edges of floors where they meet an untiled wall. Some have a coved foot, others, a coved and beaded end for finishing outside corners. All bases have at least one rounded top edge.

- *Bullnose* tile, also called cap tile, has one rounded edge. It provides a finished edge around the perimeter of field tile.

- *Down angles* and *up angles* are rounded tiles made to fit into corners.

- *V-cap edges* finish countertops.

Some manufacturers do not make trim tiles to go with their field tile. If your design won't look right without trim tile, make sure you can get it before you place your order. And be sure to budget for trim tiles—some cost twice as much as field tiles.

▼ Trim tiles are shaped to finish out the corners found in any kind of tile installation.

◀ V-cap edging will make your countertop look like it was finished by a pro. Its slightly raised profile helps keep spilled liquids on the countertop before they can get to the floor. The wide lower leg of the cap acts as an edge tile that faces the front of the countertop.

If you can't find trim to match your field tile, consider wood, metal, or PVC edging. Field tiles with rounded edges can also substitute for trim tile.

When you plan a layout with a border, be sure to include the border tiles in your sketches so you have a good idea of the final appearance.

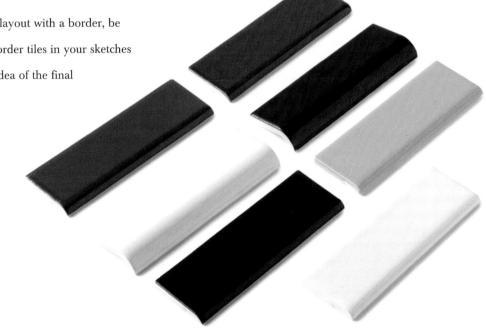

▲ Base tiles provide a stylish, colorful transition from floor tile to the walls. A tile made specifically for this purpose will feature a coved foot. Bullnose tile, with its one rounded edge, is another option. If you can't find base tiles that match your floor tiles, you can instead cut field tile, and round its edge.

DECORATIVE CERAMIC TILE

▼ When planning a project with decorative tiles, consider the grout as part of the design. Grout that matches the tiles blends in; contrasting grout makes the design stand out.

If you want to add a distinctive touch to your tile project, work decorative tiles into your design. These tiles have no other purpose than to add an attractive accent to a floor, wall, or countertop—and nothing does it better.

Decorative tiles will help show off a feature of the room (an alcove in a kitchen, for example) or create a focal point, such as a stand-alone mural or geometric inset in a floor or wall. These tiles also can bring definition to a large expanse (metal tiles as a border around ceramic field tiles) or brighten up dark spaces, such as recesses or corners in a room where the light falls off, by providing a contrasting element in the shadows.

Decorative tiles are available in ceramic, metal, glass, and other materials. Shop around for ideas that you can incorporate in your design. You might find a few styles among the tile selections at your home center, but you'll find a larger variety of these specialty items at tile retailers.

If you're looking for more unusual or one-of-a-kind decorative tiles, search the Internet for "decorative ceramic tiles" or "hand-painted tiles." Many artists have websites where you can purchase distinctive pieces. Also check with local art galleries for local ceramic artists who make tiles.

You can even find firms that will make a custom ceramic mural of almost any size from a photograph you supply. And at some ceramics shops, you can decorate your own tiles. You can paint or draw your own designs freehand or stencil tiles with color glazes and have them fired in the kiln.

Decorative tile defies rigid categorization, but the varieties fall into some broad groups:

■ *Relief tiles* are embossed or incised with a cut or stamped pattern and can add a three-dimensional appearance to your design. Their textures, however, make them more difficult to clean, so they are not a good choice for floors or backsplashes that will get greasy.

▲ Hand-painted tiles may not wear well on floors or countertops. Use them as random accents to spice up a tiled wall or backsplash.

■ *Listellos* are decorative border tiles. They make great chair rails, mural frames, and cornices, and are effective for separating a tiled wall into sections. Consider molded limestone with tumbled marble in a rustic or country setting.

■ *Antique tiles*—even those not originally intended as decorative pieces—add charm to a wall. Many will be too soft for floors or countertops, however.

■ *Murals* are tile pictures—each tile contains a section of the larger design. You might think of them only as an embellishment for walls, but they make dramatic floor accents too (be sure to use tiles rated for floors).

■ *Painted tiles* are flat field tiles or border tiles that have been decorated with glazes, then fired. The glazed finishes make the design as durable as any single-color tile.

▲ Glass tiles make wonderful accents on backsplashes, walls, and stair risers—any location where they won't get scratched easily.

▲ Search flea markets, auctions, and building-salvage sales for antique tiles. Buy the antique tiles first, then pick complementary field tiles.

STONE TILE

Stone tile brings a rich style to a room that no other material can. These tiles may be cut from slabs of stone with diamond blades and polished (gauged), or hand split (cleft) from a larger stone.

Gauged stone has one honed surface and its thickness and width are more uniform than cleft tile, which has a rougher surface. Gauged stone comes in a variety of finishes: polished, matte, or flamed—a coarse texture produced by heat.

Most varieties come in 3- to 12-inch squares, but 4×2-inch rectangles and 2-foot squares are becoming more popular. The larger sizes of tile form dramatic design elements, and their installation goes quickly. Smaller tiles are just right for floors, walls and countertops.

Marble, granite, and slate are the most popular stone tiles; but limestone, sandstone, and quartzite are becoming more popular for contemporary floors. Limestone and sandstone offer a variety of muted colors and a rough, rustic look. Varieties differ in hardness, so be sure to choose a long-wearing tile when planning a floor. Quartzite is an extremely hard and weather-resistant sandstone that comes in many colors, often in light neutral shades that fit many decorating schemes.

▲ Marble comes out of the ground in a wide range of soft hues, from nearly pure white to pure black, with pinks, grays, and greens in between.

You'll find even the hardest stone–granite–can be damaged or have color variations. When you buy stone tile, get extra tiles and examine each one for damage and color.

You can set granite almost anywhere, but other stones may not be suited to all situations. Dense, vitreous varieties of marble, for example, will stand up to hard use on floors, but soft and absorbent marbles will not. Heavily ridged slate makes for a good floor tile, but the ridges can cause stability problems on a countertop.

Stone needs a solid, smooth substrate to keep the tiles from cracking. Install stone tile on ½-inch backerboard laid over ¾-inch plywood.

▲ Granite can withstand freezing, resist staining, and stand up to heavy use. Its versatility makes it well suited for floors, walls, and countertops.

▶ You might be surprised at all the subtle variations of greens, grays, and blues that slate comes in. You can combine several colors in a quilt pattern. Its slightly ridged surface provides excellent traction on floors.

The combined thickness of underlayment, substrate, mortar, and tile will increase the height and weight of the floor. Kitchen appliances may not fit back in their bays, and bathroom doors might not close. That's why installing stone tile on a floor may require other structural adjustments. Your existing floor also may not be capable of supporting the weight of the materials. Ask a contractor to perform a deflection test to determine whether you should strengthen the floor.

One of the design characteristics peculiar to granite and marble tile is that it looks best with thin grout joints, or even none at all. Slate is attractive with grout joints up to ⅜ inch wide. Use unsanded epoxy grout so you don't scratch the tile when filling the joints.

▲ Tumbled marble or slate isn't tumbled at all. It's roughened by abrasives and acids, which brings a classic or rustic character to floors and walls. It will require sealing if used for a floor.

RESILIENTS AND LAMINATES

▲ Buy the best quality resilient tile you can afford—solid vinyl, if possible—for the longest life.

Resilient and laminate tiles offer a wide range of patterns–imitating wood, stone, and ceramic tile–at a fraction of the cost of the real thing.

Suitable only for floors, both materials come in a range of qualities and costs, so it's important to buy the best your budget will allow. Both are among the easiest of flooring materials to install–you can complete most resilient and laminate installations in a weekend.

From its earliest days, resilient tile has always taken on the appearance of other materials, and current manufacturing methods make very convincing imitations.

Resilient tile comes either dry-backed for use with mastic, or with a peel-and-stick adhesive. Both kinds of tiles should be installed over a smooth plywood subfloor; any imperfections in the subfloor will show up on the tile.

Resilient tile is made in different qualities for different budgets. The higher the vinyl content, the more costly and longer lasting the tile. Solid vinyl is more resilient, comes in more patterns, and is more expensive than vinyl composition tiles. Vinyl composition tiles usually come with self-stick backings. There are plenty of composition tile patterns to choose from, but they don't provide the low maintenance and longer wear of solid vinyl tiles.

▲ The pattern or texture on laminate tile is actually applied photographically and covered with a protective wear layer.

Laminate tiles make a more durable floor than resilient tiles, but laminates aren't quite as comfortable underfoot because they don't have the cushioning effect of resilient tile. You'll find laminates in a number of granite, marble, and stone look-alike designs, as well as abstract designs and ceramic patterns.

Laminate tile is made of layers of composite woods and plastics, fused together under high pressure and heat. Laminates bring a variety of durable design options to floors at a moderate cost—only slightly higher than resilient tile.

A tough melamine wear coat gives laminates their staying power. The top layer is as tough as the laminates used in countertops and is designed to protect the printed pattern layer below it. Most laminate flooring snaps together and should be installed over a plastic underlayment made specifically for it.

▲ Self-stick tiles are the easiest of all flooring materials to install. Just peel the protective backing off the tile and press it into place.

ANOTHER PLASTIC TILE

Vinyl tiles are the most common plastic floor tiles. Another plastic option is made from flexible polyvinyl chloride (PVC), and it's perfect to lay like a mat on garage or basement floors or any other surface you don't have the time or desire to tile permanently. These tiles have keyed edges that interlock so they won't pull apart. They come in a variety of solid bright colors and embossed patterns.

PARQUET, CORK, AND CARPET TILE

Parquet, cork, and carpet tile look different on a floor, but each combines durability with easy, do-it-yourself installation.

▲ **Parquet tile comes both prefinished and unfinished. When properly installed, both will give years of low-maintenance service.**

Parquet is a tile made from glued wood pieces. It comes either unfinished or with a factory-applied finish, with flat or beveled edges. Parquet tiles are usually 12-inch squares, although other shapes are available.

The standard wood-strip pattern on each square tile is parallel, with variations of grain in several of the pieces that provide some visual texture. Many other patterns are available to create the look of an expensive inlaid floor. You'll find rectangular and triangular patterns, rhomboids, interlocking triangles, and three-dimensional patterns. You can buy parquet tiles at flooring shops or through Internet websites.

If you treat a high-quality unfinished parquet with a penetrating sealer and an annual waxing—or with a polyurethane varnish—it will last for years. A prefinished floor with a factory-applied polyurethane won't need regular waxing. Keep it fresh with a vacuum and recoat it every five or six years.

Before you decide what to buy, inspect the finish carefully. If the finish has bubbles, dust, paper bits, swirls or sander marks, or if the wood strips feel loose or look wavy, choose another tile.

Cork tile costs more than parquet and carpet tile, but it offers textures, natural patterns, and a

▲ **Cork tile is usually considered a floor covering, but don't overlook its potential for a noise-reducing wallcovering.**

soft feel underfoot because of tiny air cells in the cork. These cells also allow cork to absorb and deaden sound effectively. The cells help make the floor feel warm in the winter and cool in the summer too. Cork's natural resilience lets it bounce back from dents.

No two cork tiles are alike—each displays a unique color, pattern, and texture. Cork is a renewable flooring material—it's cut from the cork oak, which regenerates its bark about every nine years.

Carpet tile is usually made in 18-inch squares of various thicknesses, and in hundreds of weave and pattern appearances. Like resilient products, this tile is sold either as a dry-back tile for mastic application or as a self-stick tile. Carpet tile can be laid with a permanent adhesive or with a releasable mastic, which allows easy removal of damaged tiles.

Carpet tile was considered a second-rate flooring material for a long time, but new fibers and manufacturing methods have improved its quality, environmental safety, and durability.

Low cost is not the only attractive characteristic of self-stick carpet tile. Aside from peel-and-stick resilient tile, nothing goes on faster than self-stick carpet tile. You will

◀ **Damaged or worn carpet tiles can be replaced with little effort.**

probably be able to lay out and install a 10×12-foot room in a couple of hours.

Carpet tile also lends itself to more design variations than might at first be apparent. You can create different patterns by orienting the pile of the fabric (the direction of its weave, indicated by arrows on the back of the tiles) in different ways. Arrange the tiles to look like broadloom carpet or lay them out in a figured pattern, which is an effective way to minimize the appearance of wear.

All of these materials—parquet, cork, and carpet—need to be installed over a smooth plywood subfloor.

WHAT GOES UNDERNEATH?

All tile must be installed on a sound, stable, and smooth base. You can install non-mortared tile on smooth plywood, but ceramic and stone tile need something more substantial.

You can install ceramic tile over concrete, drywall, or plaster surfaces, but not plywood.

Plywood draws water out of mortar, and it expands faster than tile, which increases the chances of cracked joints. Some installations call for a stronger substrate, such as backerboard.

Here are some standard substrates used with ceramic and stone tile.

Drywall, a gypsum core compressed between two layers of heavy paper, is a good substrate for walls that won't get wet. It comes in 4×8 and larger sheets. Drywall that's ½ inch thick is suitable for most walls.

Greenboard is drywall with a water-resistant covering. It's available in 4×8 sheets; ½-inch and ⅝-inch sheets are usually used on walls. It's good in areas that won't constantly get wet, but it won't stand up to constant water exposure.

Backerboard comes in several forms and is the preferred substrate for tile installations in both wet and dry locations.

Greenboard

Cement-backerboard

Gypsum-based backerboard

Concrete slab

Drywall (gypsum wallboard)

Plywood

◀ Tile can be laid over many materials, but some substrates are not suitable for some types of tile. Your tile dealer can help you decide on the best substrate for your tile. Backerboard is usually the best substrate for a durable tile surface.

Backerboard is made from cement and fiberglass, gypsum and fiberglass, or cement and cellulose additives. It is the best substrate for ceramic or stone tile. It comes in sheets of various lengths and widths; ½-inch boards are the most common thickness for floors, walls, and countertops.

To tile a concrete slab, you'll probably need an *isolation membrane,* a *waterproofing membrane,* or both. Isolation membrane, a liquid material, keeps cracks from telegraphing into the tile. You'll also need a waterproofing membrane for tub and shower enclosures.

Ask your tile supplier about the best substrate for your installation.

▼ Self-leveling compounds are used to level depressions in slabs and subfloors. Quick-setting brands allow tiling within hours.

SUBSTRATES FOR CERAMIC TILE

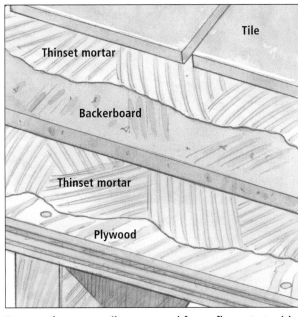

Tile

Thinset mortar

Backerboard

Thinset mortar

Plywood

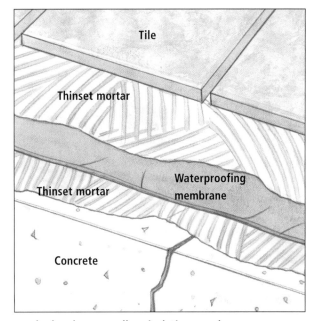

Tile

Thinset mortar

Waterproofing membrane

Thinset mortar

Concrete

To properly support tile on a wood frame floor, start with ¾-inch exterior plywood underlayment, followed by ½-inch backerboard, mortar, and the tile. A concrete slab will need a brush-on or roll-on isolation membrane over cracks and a waterproofing membrane to keep moisture from wicking up into the mortar.

ADHESIVES, GROUTS, CAULKS, AND SEALERS

Tile, except for some laminate tile, needs some kind of adhesive to attach to its substrate (see *page 164)*. Self-stick resilient and carpet tiles come from the factory with adhesive on the back. Thinset mortars and organic mastics are made for ceramic tile and stone.

Ceramic tile and most stone tile require grout to fill the joints in addition to the mortar underneath. Grout comes in many colors and usually falls into one of two categories—sanded and unsanded grout. Sanded grout is used for most installations, but use unsanded grout when tiling with stone.

Both thinset mortars and grouts come premixed or dry for mixing with water. Some projects—especially those in outdoor or wet areas—require a latex additive in the mix.

Thinset and other adhesives contain caustic ingredients, and solvent-base adhesives are potentially explosive and harmful when inhaled. Wear gloves and a respirator when mixing all adhesives and keep the area well ventilated.

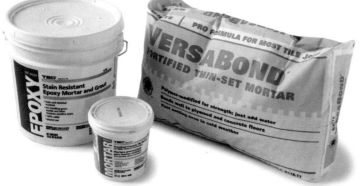
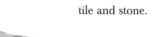

▲ Most adhesives are made for a specific tile and installation. Be sure to choose the product appropriate to your materials.

A variety of solvent-base mastics are manufactured for parquet, resilient tile, cork, and carpet tile. Some laminate tiles snap together and are made to float on a plastic underlayment without being adhered to the floor. Some laminates can be glued at their edges to provide a waterproof seal in wet areas, such as bathroom floors.

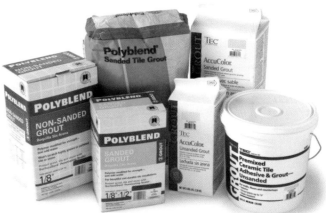

▲ Grouts are tough and durable but not waterproof. Seal the grout lines to keep them from staining or being damaged by water or other liquids.

▶ Flexible caulks seal the edges of a tiled installation, primarily at the joint of the perimeter of a floor or patio, at the joint between a countertop and backsplash, and over control joints in a concrete slab. Sealers prevent staining and moisture damage to the tiled surface.

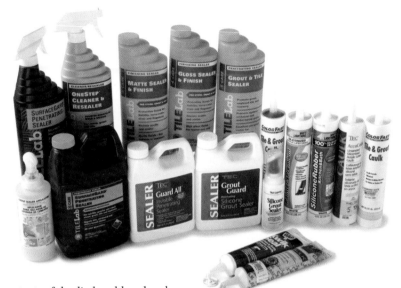

Caulking is often overlooked as a necessary tiling material, probably because it occupies so little of the tiled area. Caulks are essential, however, where a flexible seal is required to keep water out and let the materials expand and contract without breaking the tile or joints. Fill larger gaps with foam backer rod or expansion joint

Sealers are usually applied as the last step in a tile application. They protect soft-bodied and handmade tile and stone tile (and their grout lines) from staining and damage. Like other tiling products, they are made for specific types of tile. Follow the manufacturer's instructions when choosing a sealer and its applicator.

USING FOAM BACKER ROD

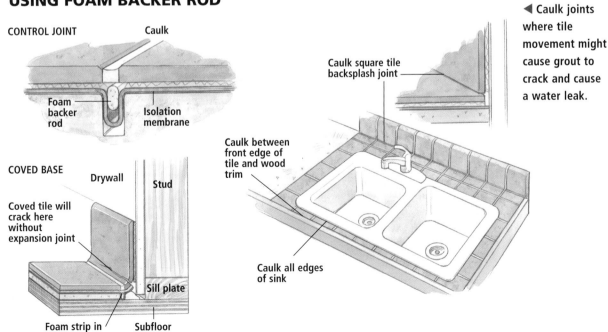

CONTROL JOINT

Caulk

Foam backer rod

Isolation membrane

COVED BASE

Drywall

Stud

Coved tile will crack here without expansion joint

Sill plate

Foam strip in expansion joint

Subfloor

Caulk square tile backsplash joint

Caulk between front edge of tile and wood trim

Caulk all edges of sink

◀ Caulk joints where tile movement might cause grout to crack and cause a water leak.

MAKING PLANS

You can install tile successfully without a detailed plan, but you'll find the job goes a lot easier and is less time consuming—and your results will be more professional looking—if you draw up a plan.

A well-drawn plan does more than keep your tile in line. It will also make your material estimates and budget projections more accurate and provide you with a basis for organizing the work in sections. A plan also will help you communicate with contractors you hire for any part of the work. In some areas, especially for outdoor installations, the local building department may require a detailed plan. If you seek a permit without a detailed plan, officials will send you back to the drawing board.

▼ **A detailed drawing for a kitchen floor should include the dimensions of appliance space. When you note floor dimensions, be sure to account for the removal of baseboards but not toe-kicks under the cabinets.**

Make a rough sketch of the room or area. Then start in a corner and measure, to the nearest ⅛ inch, the length of every surface. Write the measurements on the sketch as you go.

Include the location and dimensions of windows, doors, appliances, and plumbing fixtures, such as toilets, sinks, tubs, and showers. A sketch of a wall or countertop should include anything on the surface that interrupts a line of tile, such as a window, electrical outlet, or switch.

DIMENSIONAL KITCHEN DRAWING

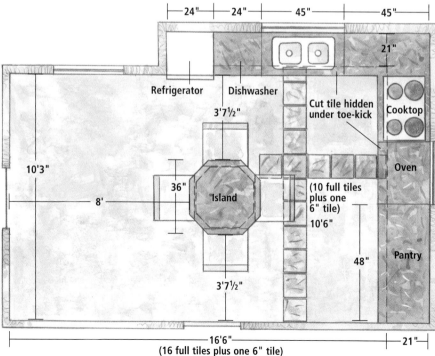

Once you've completed the sketch and its measurements, transfer the information to a scaled drawing of the installation. On graph paper, draw the perimeter of the room to scale with a ruler and drafting tools. Then add the measurements and label the major features of the installation.

Because this drawing will provide you with the basis for making final layout decisions, choose a scale that's appropriate for the size of the tile you will use. A drawing scaled so ¼ inch equals 1 foot may be perfect for 12-inch tiles, but too small for 4- to 6-inch tiles. Smaller tiles are easier to render on a larger scale.

When your paper plans are completed, you can consider the one aspect of planning that the drawing can't solve—the disruption of the family schedule that a tiling project can cause.

If the kitchen will be unavailable, make alternate arrangements for meals. Coordinate the removal of bathroom fixtures with your family's daily schedule.

DRAWING THE LAYOUT

The level of detail required for a scaled drawing will depend somewhat on the nature of the installation. You'll probably need to tape tracing paper over your scaled drawing and experiment with various tile layouts. If you don't like one, start another on a fresh sheet of tracing paper. Better to get the layout right now than discover problems after you've troweled on the mortar.

DIMENSIONAL BATHROOM DRAWING

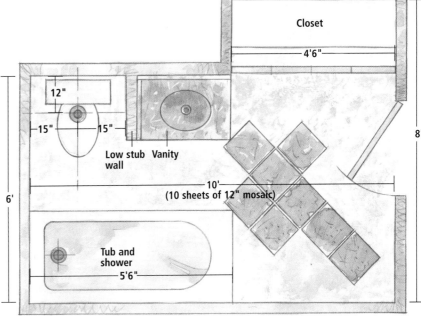

▲ To ensure sufficient detail for a bathroom plan, measure the location of the toilet flange as accurately as possible. The toilet will still be in place when you draw the plan, but the flange will be hidden. To find the position of the flange, measure from the sidewall to half the width of the toilet base and from the back wall to about one-fourth of its length.

CHAPTER HIGHLIGHTS

This chapter shows the techniques for installing ceramic and stone tile, as well as parquet, laminates, cork, and resilient and carpet tile, on floors. It also shows how to install mosaic and border tile on a floor.

TILING FLOORS

All kinds of tile require a smooth and stable surface, whether the surface is wood or a concrete slab. General preparation steps for tiling are discussed in Chapter 8. The chapter's sections show how different surfaces and different kinds of tile may require additional preparation. If your floor is 1×4 planking, for example, you should overlay it with backerboard for ceramic and stone tile and plywood for other types.

You can lay ceramic tile over hardwood flooring and existing ceramic tile if the surface is sound and the subfloor is in good condition. The same is true for uncushioned resilient tile, laminates, parquet, and carpet tile. Ceramic and stone tile, however, may add enough weigh that you have to reinforce the floor structure.

Make sure the tile you buy is suitable for your project; some tile is suitable to lay on a concrete slab that's at or below grade, but some can be installed only above grade. Before installing tile on a concrete slab, cover cracks with an isolation membrane and install a waterproofing membrane, or use a combination membrane.

Whatever kind of tile you plan to install, get thorough instructions from your dealer or home center about the steps you need to take to prepare for the installation. Store tile and other materials in the room where they will be installed so they can adjust to the temperature and humidity. All tiles show some color variation from lot to lot. Mix cartons together before you start to spread the variations across the entire surface.

TILING AN ENTRYWAY

Entryways are often the smallest spaces in a home, but they may be the most-used space in the house, sustaining the constant coming and going of household members. They withstand wet shoes, cold blasts from winter winds, and constant wear and tear. Ceramic and stone tile stand up well to the rigors of an entryway floor, and provide a visual transition between the outdoors and the rest of the rooms in the house.

Tile is also good to use there because for all their prominence in a home design, entryways are often the least attractive space. A strong tile pattern can brighten up a drab entryway. Because the area is small, you can splurge a bit on borders and inset tiles; a stylish layout won't cost you a fortune in an entryway.

Be sure to use unglazed tiles so your floor won't get slippery when it's wet. Machined or handmade pavers are a good choice. So is slate, which has an irregular surface that provides some natural traction. If your plans include a tiled surface outside the house, use the same material inside to make a smooth transition. Choose colors that complement the colors of the flooring in the rooms. An entryway can open to several rooms, so lay it out to look its best from where it will most often be seen.

If you're using backerboard, insert a foam backer rod into the gap between the backerboard and the wall (see *page 37*). Tile and backerboard will raise the level of the floor so you may need to raise the threshold and cut the bottom of the entry door. A substrate of felt and metal lath (see *opposite page*) may keep the floor height low enough to avoid this adjustment.

▼ **Layout becomes a little more complex with decorative tiles. Mark the position of the decorative inserts and snap lines in both directions at each point where the pattern or the tile size changes.**

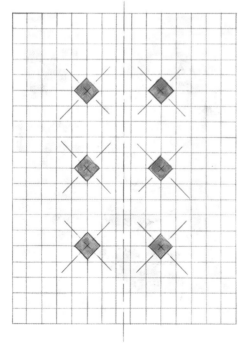

LAYING THE TILE

1 Dry-lay the tiles to test your layout. Then snap as many layout lines as the pattern needs (see *pages 160–161*). Start at the door and trowel on thinset (see *pages 164–167*). Set field tile first with the edges on the layout lines. Insert spacers as you go, and check the sections with a straightedge. Clean excess mortar from the joints by dragging a spacer between the tiles.

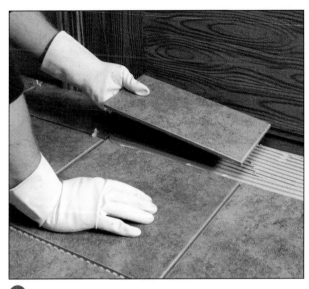

2 When the mortar under the field tiles is dry (usually overnight), cut and lay the edge tile (see *pages 168–169*). Round the cut edges with a masonry stone to give them a finished appearance. Clean the joints and let the mortar dry before you grout the tiles.

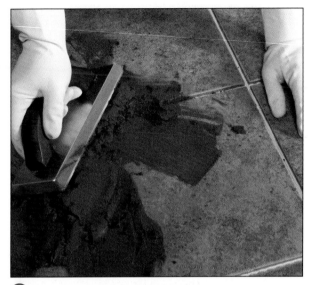

3 Apply a small amount of grout onto the tile—enough to cover a section you can work before the grout sets up. Force grout into the joint with a grout float, let it set slightly, then scrape the excess from the surface. Clean the grout from the surface and wipe off the haze with rags. Finish the joint at the wall with matching caulk.

4 If the threshold wasn't installed before the tile, cut the threshold to fit the doorway, and install it with fasteners recommended by the manufacturer.

BUILDING A BASE OF METAL LATH AND FELT

1 On a firm, solid plywood subfloor, staple 15-pound felt paper, overlapping the edges by 2 or 3 inches. Then staple metal lath to the floor, butting (not overlapping) the edges.

2 Mix bedding mortar (half portland cement, half fine sand) and trowel it over the lath ¼ inch deep. Smooth the surface and let it cure. Knock off any high spots, then spread thinset and lay the tile.

TILING A FLOOR BORDER

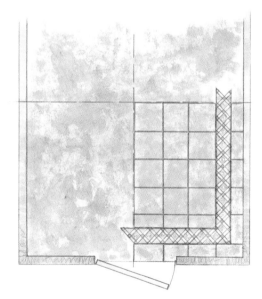

Borders can turn what could otherwise be a mundane tile installation into a stunning design element, and the array of border styles is almost endless.

The easiest to install are mesh-backed mosaic strips, where the manufacturer has already taken care of the cutting and arranging the pattern. But you can design your own border from loose tiles, stone tiles, or glass tiles. The key to a good design is selecting a color and pattern that complements the color, pattern, and texture of your field tiles. Borders work well on an entryway floor, where the small area allows you to take in the design in one glance.

One of the key decisions is whether to install the border against the wall or outline the border with a row of edge tiles. It's usually better to keep cut tiles along the wall, not within the border tile.

LAYING THE TILE

Space for edge tiles equal on opposite walls

Cardboard template cut to width of border

1 As shown on *page 47,* snap chalk lines at the midpoints of opposite walls and square them, using the 3-4-5 triangle *(page 160).* Dry-lay tiles on each axis, using a cardboard template as a place holder for the border. Move the tile lines until you have even tiles at both ends along the outside edge of the border. Repeat on the other axis. Measure and snap layout lines (see *pages 160–161).*

▼ Layout is crucial to setting a tile border. Draw a precise dimensional plan, allowing for the likelihood that the room is not square.

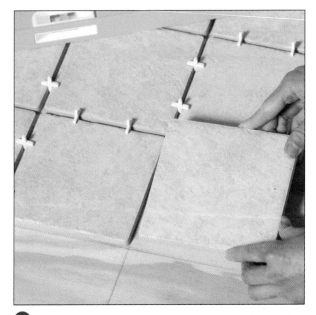

2 Start at the intersection of your centered lines and lay the tile in two adjacent quadrants. This will complete the field tiles along one wall. Line up the tiles in each section with a metal straightedge. Lay the field tiles in the remaining quadrants and let the mortar dry.

3 If you're laying a mesh-backed border, dry-lay the border strip and adjust its position so that any cuts you make at the end of the border strip will fall in line with a grout line in the field tiles. Use the same method with individual border tiles, adjusting their position until the cut lines correspond to the field-tile grout lines.

4 Spread thinset in the border recess and lay the border tiles. Adjust all the tiles to space them evenly and line them up along the edges. Seat the tiles with a beater block as you would any mosaic tile (see *page 51*). Then measure, cut, and set the edge tiles. Let the mortar cure.

5 Mix as much grout as you can apply before it sets up. Force the grout between the tiles with a grout float, removing any excess from the surface of each section before grouting the next (see *page 171*). When the grout has set, clean the tile with a dampened sponge and wipe off the remaining haze.

TILING A KITCHEN FLOOR

Kitchens pose a number of layout challenges not encountered in other rooms. First, because they often are not rectangular, your first challenge will be to decide where to snap the first set of layout lines. It's usually best to snap them at the midpoints of the largest open rectangular area (see illustration, *opposite*). In L-shaped kitchens, you may need to start with two sets of lines.

Toe-kicks and cabinets are another element not found in most other rooms. Although you may not have to remove the base cabinets and tile under them, the combined thickness of tile, mortar, and substrate can significantly reduce the toe-kick space. You may need to remove the cabinets and tile under them or raise the floor beneath the cabinet area with additional underlayment. You should remove appliances, including undercounter ones, and tile under them. Removing and raising the cabinets will eliminate the need to notch the countertops so undercounter appliances will fit onto the new floor height.

Plywood can serve as a suitable substrate, but your tiled floor will be much less likely to crack if you use cement backerboard. Stuff foam backer rod in between the outside edge of the backerboard and the wall (see *page 37*). Leave doors that swing out of the room in place, but remove inswinging doors if needed.

LAYING THE TILE

1 Snap and square center lines between the midpoints of the walls or the largest open rectangular space on the floor (see illustration, *below*, and *page 160).* Then snap layout lines at the dimensions of your tile and a grout joint. If you're including a border, snap lines where the field tile ends and the border begins. Dry-lay the tiles to space the edges evenly. For complicated borders, set the tile on cardboard and trace its outline. Cut out the pattern and use this stencil to lightly spray-paint the pattern on the floor.

2 Laying the toe-kick tiles first will prove easier than trying to slide them into place next to a field tile. Or, you can begin laying tiles from the intersection of any layout lines, but when you get within one tile of the toe-kick, lay the edge before completing the field-tile row. The cut edges of the tile will be hidden under the toe-kick. Set the factory edge toward the field tile.

LAYING OUT DIFFERENT FLOOR PLANS

RECTANGULAR ROOM

Chalk lines at midpoints of walls

L-SHAPE ROOM

Chalk lines

Doorway

DIAGONAL LAYOUT

Chalk lines

5'

5'

▲ Where you snap your layout lines depends on the shape of the kitchen. These illustrations show the starting points for some common layouts.

3 Lay the tiles with spacers, if necessary, and embed them with a beater block (see *page 167*). As you complete each section of the floor, check all edges with a straightedge and push the tiles in line before tiling the next section. Use a carpenter's level to check for high and low tiles and reset them (see *page 167*). Continue laying tile and inserting spacers, cleaning excess thinset from the joints as you go. Let the mortar cure, then cut tiles for the remaining edges and set them.

4 Mix enough grout to cover a section of the floor. Starting in a corner opposite a doorway, pack grout into the joints with a grout float (see *page 45*). Let the grout set up—when a damp sponge won't pull it from the joint, it's ready to be cleaned. Scrape the excess off the tile with the float and use a damp sponge to remove the residue (see *page 171*). Then damp-sponge again. When the surface dries, wipe off the haze with a dry rag. Caulk the perimeter joint.

ADDING A TILE BASE

1 Your floor might not be level, but your tile base should be. Set the bullnose tile against the wall with spacers (no mortar). Adjust each tile with plastic wedges until all their top edges are level. Stand back and study the joint at the bottom of the tile base. It should not look too thick. Readjust the tiles if necessary. When all the tiles around the perimeter of the room are level, run a pencil line along the top edge at the corners.

2 Remove the tiles and snap a level chalk line between the corner marks. Then mix up enough thinset to cover the area where you'll be working. Back-butter each tile and set it in place.

3 Press each tile in place with a slight twist, inserting spacers and nudging one tile against the spacer before setting the next one. Keep the tile level along the line by inserting plastic wedges as you go. Then to make sure (and because it's difficult to get things level at the bottom of a wall), check the tile with a carpenter's level and adjust the tile if necessary by pushing or pulling on the wedges. Gently remove excess mortar from the joints with a spacer and wipe the surface clean. Set and clean the corner tiles, let the mortar cure overnight, then grout and clean the border. Caulk the joint at the floor and along the top edge of the trim. Smooth the caulk with a wet finger or sponge.

CUTTING YOUR OWN BASE TILES

1 Some manufacturers do not make bullnose tile to match the field tile. If bullnose is not available, you can cut your own base tiles. First decide how tall you want the base tiles to be, then cut field tiles to this width. When you cut the base tile from a large floor tile, keep the factory edge. Install the base tiles with the factory edge on top.

2 Install the cut tile and, if the factory edge is not finished the way you want it to be, grout the top edge and clean the excess from the walls before it dries.

Installing Mosaic Tile

Mesh-backed and dot-mounted sheets take the trouble out of tiling with mosaics. Properly spaced individual tiles adhere to a backing so you don't have to set each tile one at a time.

If you're using dot-mounted sheets, check the back of the tile for any oily film that might be left over from the manufacturing process. Adhesive won't stick to the film, so clean it with a mild detergent solution.

Plain mosaics with a single color and with no pattern are quicker to lay out than a patterned installation. That's because you won't have to dry-lay the sheets to create even borders at the edges. Because all the mosaics look the same, you won't notice uneven borders. You will have to dry-lay a patterned mosaic, however, which might require you to cut the pattern at the edges. To avoid a cut pattern (which is certain to look unprofessional), either select tile with a design that will fit the room without cutting the pattern or consider using solid tile as a border around the room.

Carefully install mosaics with random geometric patterns. Make sure the color schemes throughout the design don't look haphazard. Dry-lay the sheets and adjust their position until you get a balanced arrangement across the surface of the floor. Then number them so you can set them in the same order.

To fit mosaics around pipes and obstacles, cut the mesh with a utility knife. If you have to cut an individual piece, strip it from the backing, cut it with nippers, and back-butter it with thinset before setting it.

Mortar is bound to seep into the joints and cause your grout to look mottled, so use an epoxy mortar for both the adhesive and the grout.

LAYING THE TILE

1 Snap layout lines at the midpoints of the walls (see *page 160*) and spread epoxy thinset up to—but not over—the lines. Line up the corners of the mosaic sheet with the lines and lay the sheet. Embed the sheet with a beater block and rubber mallet. Make sure the entire sheet is level in the mortar—the small pieces show an uneven surface easily.

2 Using the same techniques, lay the next and subsequent sheets. When you embed the sheets with the beater block, make sure all the edges are level.

3 As you lay the first three or four sheets, pull each one up and check it for full coverage. If even a few tiles are bare, lay the sheet face down on a clean surface and skim more mortar on the back. Recomb the mortar on the floor and reset the sheet with the beater block. After a section or two, you'll get used to spreading the right amount of mortar.

4 Continue setting the tiles in sections, using a metal straightedge to keep your layout straight. Wipe up excess mortar with a damp (not wet) sponge. Let the mortar set, then grout and clean the tiles.

INSTALLING STONE TILE

Stone tile can fracture along its grain, so it needs a solid substrate. Install it on a floor prepared with ¾-inch underlayment and cement backerboard.

Stone tiles won't be as perfect as machine-made ceramic tile. Stone is a natural material, and some tiles might be slightly wider or thinner than others. If so, you can make adjustments when you set the tile. Trim wider pieces to the standard size or reserve them to cut for the edges. Back-butter more mortar on thin tiles to bring them level with the rest. Use white thinset on marble and other translucent tiles; gray mortar will show through. Make sure that all the edges of the tile are on the same line—check often with a carpenter's level.

Most manufacturers bevel the edges of stone tiles. So when you cut a tile, hone the cut edge with a masonry stone to make the cut edge look like the other edges. If you don't have a masonry stone, use a carpenter's sanding block. You can polish the edge (or the surface) of stone tile with progressively finer grits of carbide sandpaper (from 120- to 600-grit or finer). Use the same techniques to round the edges and make bullnose tile, if it isn't available to buy.

Cut straight edges on stone tile with a wet saw; don't try to use a snap cutter on stone. Cut holes when necessary with a dry-cutting saw and a diamond blade. Knock out the middle of the cut with nippers.

LAYING THE TILE

1 Wipe your finger across the back of the tile; if you can see the path of your finger on the back of the tile, clean the dust off with a wet sponge. Let the tiles dry before laying them.

2 Lay out the tiles in a dry run and adjust their position until the edge tiles are the same size (see *page 44*). Then snap layout lines that correspond to the dimensions of your tile and one grout line. Trowel thinset on the subfloor and back-butter the tile. Set and level the field tiles, back-buttering additional mortar as needed. Line up the edges of the tile with a straightedge.

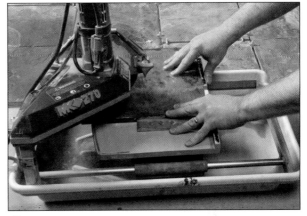

3 When the field tiles have set overnight, cut the edge tiles with a wet saw and lay them in a mortar bed, back-buttering each tile as you go. If the width of one tile differs more than ⅛ inch from the others, you may have to measure and cut each tile separately.

4 Let the edge tiles cure for 24 hours. Then mix just enough unsanded grout to cover a small section. Stone tiles can absorb a lot of water from the grout, so mist the edges with a spray bottle. Apply the grout in sections (see *page 48*), cleaning each section before the excess hardens. When the grout has completely cured, seal the surface.

INSTALLING DRY-BACK RESILIENT TILE

The variety of resilient tile adhesives can seem confusing at first. Each adhesive is made for a specific application—some for concrete slabs, for unbacked tile, for a wood floor above grade, and others for a wood floor below grade. Ask your tile supplier to recommend an adhesive for the tile you're using and for the surface on which you'll lay it.

Most resilient adhesives are solvent-base. They go on thin but have a tendency to cause the trowel to stick to the surface as you're spreading them—a tendency you'll quickly learn to overcome. Many solvent-base adhesives are volatile and hazardous when breathed, so open a window, put an exhaust fan in a window, and wear a respirator for complete safety.

On the back of some resilient tile you'll see an arrow that shows the direction of the grain in the tile, a grain that's almost invisible, but that will affect the appearance of your floor. For a consistent appearance, set the tiles with the grain running in the same direction. You can give the floor a distinctive look by laying tiles with the arrows in different directions, but dry-lay the tiles first to make sure you like the effect.

Almost all resilients—grained or ungrained—have a pattern. For the best look, pay close attention to the pattern and lay it appropriately. If you want to experiment with changing the layout of the pattern, dry-lay the tiles first.

In addition to the pattern, the colors should be consistent. Ask your retailer to give you tiles from the same dye lots. If that's not possible, open three cartons at a time and mix the tiles into a single batch so any color variations will spread randomly across the floor.

LAYING THE TILE

1 Lay out the room as shown on *page 47*. Then, starting at the intersection of the layout lines, spread adhesive with the smooth edge of a notched trowel. Do not cover the lines. Then comb the adhesive with the notched edge. Let the adhesive set up until it's tacky.

2 Set the corner of the first tile on the intersection of the layout lines and lower it into the adhesive. Then check the grain direction of the next tile and set it against the first one. Push the edge of each succeeding tile against one that's already laid, then lower the new tile into place. Avoid sliding the tiles so you don't push mastic up between the joints. Continue setting the quadrant.

3 To mark the perimeter tiles for cutting, set a loose tile exactly on top of the last tile in a row. Then set a marker tile on top of that one, positioning it on the wall against ¼-inch spacers. Be sure to keep the grain pattern consistent. Run a pencil along the edge of the marker tile to mark the cut line.

4 When you have finished the first quadrant, clean off adhesive that may have seeped through the joints, using the solvent recommended by the manufacturer (usually detergent and water). Don't wet the floor; excess liquid weakens water-base adhesives. Roll the entire floor after all the quadrants and edge tiles are in place.

CUTTING RESILIENT TILE

1 Soften the tile along the cut line slightly with a hair dryer.

2 Score the cut line with a utility knife. Make repeated passes until you cut through the tile. For cut edges that will be hidden by molding or toe-kicks, you can snap the tile after a few passes with the knife.

INSTALLING SELF-STICK VINYL TILE

You can lay out peel-and-stick tile the same way you would other resilient tile, but installation is unlike dry-back tiles. Some self-stick brands require a primer on the floor, especially if your substrate is porous.

But the most important difference is that the adhesive won't budge once it contacts the floor. You can't reposition a self-stick tile as you can one laid with mortar or mastic. So positioning the first tile exactly on the intersection of the layout lines is crucial. Get the first one right and the rest should be easy. You can remove a misplaced tile, but prying it up will break it to pieces. Be sure to order a few extra tiles to allow for some misplacements.

Dispose of the paper backings in a bag or bucket as soon as you pull each one from a tile. These thin paper sheets are extremely slippery and can cause a bad fall.

LAYING THE TILE

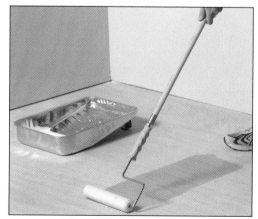

1 Follow the manufacturer's instructions to prime the floor, if required. Unless otherwise recommended by the instructions, apply two coats of primer. Apply a thin first coat, then roll on the second coat full strength.

2 Using the methods shown on *pages 160–161*, snap chalk lines between the midpoints of opposite walls to locate the center of the room. Square the lines with a 3-4-5 triangle and dry-lay the tiles along each axis (keep the backing on) until you have tiles of equal width around the edges, then snap layout lines.

3 Set out the tiles loosely along the layout lines with the grain arrows (on the backing) facing in the same or opposite directions (depending on how you want the pattern to look). Peel away the paper backing slowly and dispose of it. Set the corner of the tile at the intersection of the layout lines and press it down. Stick it firmly by rolling it with a small roller.

CUTTING SELF-STICK TILE

4 Continue setting the tiles, keeping the grain direction consistent and making sure each one butts squarely against the adjoining tiles on two sides. If you mistakenly lay a tile with the wrong orientation, immediately soften the adhesive with a hair dryer and pry up the tile with a putty knife.

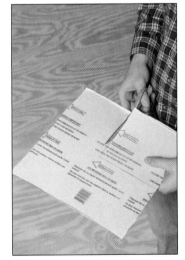

1 Leave the backing on the tile while marking and cutting it. Use a heavy-duty household scissors to cut the tile along the lines.

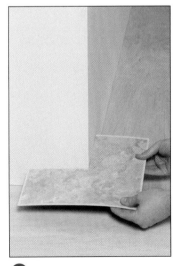

2 Peel off the backing and dispose of it. Position the edges of the tile carefully against adjacent tiles before you press it into place.

INSTALLING PARQUET TILE

Unlike many other kinds of tile, priced according to size, thickness, and pattern, the range of parquet prices reflects wide quality differences, so buy the best you can afford. Inexpensive parquet often has tongue-and-groove edges that don't fit precisely, binding agents that don't keep the strips together, and finishes that won't stand up to hard use. Ill-fitting and cheaply made tiles quickly show gaps and curled edges and often come apart when you cut them.

The placement of the first 10 to 12 tiles is critical to the success of your project. So are tight joints. Tap each joint with a hammer and a piece of scrap tile inserted into the tongue or groove to seat the tiles securely. At the edges of the room, leave a ¼-inch gap between the tile and the walls.

If you need to work from a tiled area to one that's untiled, kneel on plywood squares (using knee pads). Cut two squares so you can move one while you're kneeling on the other, and work your way across the floor.

LAYING THE TILE

1 Snap and square chalk lines between the midpoints of the walls to locate the center of the room (see *pages 160–161*). Dry-lay the tiles to make sure you have edge tiles of the same width, and adjust the lines again if necessary. Position a cork expansion strip along the wall.

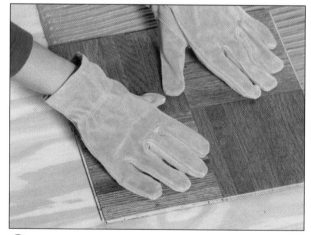

2 Spread mortar up to but not over the layout lines, letting it become tacky if recommended by the manufacturer. Then set the corner of the first tile on the intersection of the lines and lower it into the adhesive. Use the edge of the tile—not the tongue—to line up the tile. Don't slide the tile—you'll push up the adhesive into the joint, making it difficult to achieve tight joints.

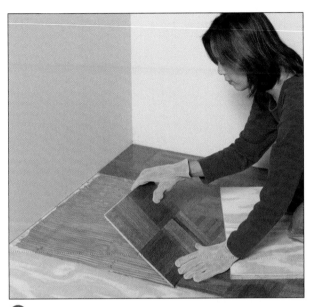

3 With the second tile slightly raised, insert the tongue into the groove of the first tile and press it down and in. Continue laying the parquet in the first quadrant. When you have to work on the surface of the tile, support your weight with a 2×2-foot plywood sheet. Mark the edge tiles for cutting and cut them on a tablesaw (finished side up).

4 Use the same technique to install the tiles in the remaining quadrants, always beginning a section next to tiles already in place and at the intersection of the layout lines. Roll each section with a 100-pound floor roller. Most adhesives require rolling within four hours of application.

SETTING PARQUET ON THE DIAGONAL

Mark the floor with diagonal layout lines. Spread and comb mortar in one of the quadrants and lay the first tile square against the intersection of the lines. Set tiles using the techniques shown on these pages.

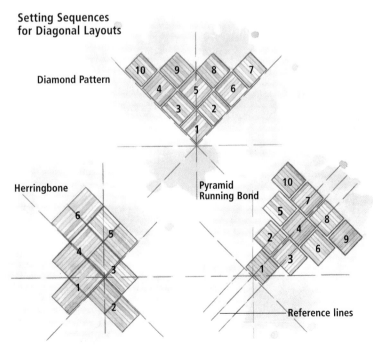

Setting Sequences for Diagonal Layouts

Diamond Pattern

Herringbone

Pyramid Running Bond

Reference lines

Installing Cork Tile

Cork tile is porous, so it requires more time to acclimate than other tiles. You should bring it into the room three or four days before you begin the installation. Imperfections in the subfloor show through the tile readily, so make sure you prepare a smooth surface.

If possible, snap your layout lines before you bring the tiles into the room. That way, you can open the cartons, mix the tiles together to spread any natural variations in texture across the floor, and set the tile in batches close to your layout sections. Cork will acclimate much more evenly when taken out of its cartons.

The adhesive used to lay cork tile is a reciprocal adhesive, commonly called contact cement. That means it only sticks to itself (one coat is spread on the floor, the other coat is on the tile). But when it sticks, it sticks permanently. Be especially careful when lining up cork tiles because you won't be able to nudge an out-of-place tile into position. You can pry up a mislaid tile (see *opposite page*), but doing so will break it into pieces, and cork is not cheap.

Some manufacturers recommend priming the subfloor before applying the adhesive. Most cork-tile adhesives are water-base, so you can remove stray adhesive from the walls with a wet sponge. If it dries, scrub it off gently with a nylon dish scrubber.

Cork tile looks better with offset joints every other row, like a brick wall. The easiest way to achieve a consistent offset is to snap a different-color line half a tile width from your first layout lines, as shown in Step 1.

When you've finished laying the tile, seal the cork with an applicator or mop. Reseal it periodically, as recommended by the manufacturer. Put the resealing schedule on your maintenance calendar.

LAYING THE TILE

1 Snap and square layout lines in the center of the room (see *page 160)*. Then, using a different chalk color, snap a parallel line on each side of your centerline, one-half a tile width from it. These second lines will help you offset the joints accurately.

2 Starting along the walls, apply the adhesive with a brush or trowel, depending on the manufacturer's recommendation. Avoid splashing adhesive on the wall. Then fill in the rest of the quadrant. Let the adhesive become tacky.

3 Set the corner of the first tile on the intersection of the lines and lower it into place, keeping its edges squared to the layout lines.

4 Set one edge of the second tile against the edge of the first tile, then lower it into place, keeping the bottom edge on the layout line. Tap both tiles with a rubber mallet and a carpet-covered beater block (see *page 51)*. Continue setting the remaining tiles in the row. Start the next row on the offset lines and proceed across the quadrant, working from installed tile to the corner. After two rows, you'll probably have to work from the tile. Don't worry about kneeling on the tile—you won't dislodge it. Lay all the field tile in this quadrant, then cut and lay the edge tile. Use the same techniques to finish the remaining quadrants. Seal the entire floor according to the manufacturer's instructions.

LIFTING A MISALIGNED TILE

If you lay a cork tile incorrectly, you can remove it by sliding a wide putty knife under a corner and working it back and forth while prying up the tile. Reapply the adhesive and set in another tile—you probably won't be able to remove cork tile in one piece.

Installing Carpet Tile

Like resilient tile, carpet tile is available as dry-back and self-stick varieties. The dry-back tile (which is thicker and more durable) requires a coat of mastic adhesive, or it can be installed with double-face carpet tape. Mastic results in a more permanent installation, and you can adjust the tiles more easily than you can with tape, but taped tile is easier to remove, a factor you may want to consider if the carpet tile is a temporary installation.

Both kinds of carpet tile are manufactured with their pile running in a particular direction, which is indicated by arrows on the back. You don't have to keep the arrows pointing in the same direction, but you should keep the pattern of their orientation consistent. Some piles look better with the arrows pointing to the same wall (resulting in more of a broadloom look). Others will look better with the pile going in opposite directions. Arranging the arrows in four

directions will produce square sections of pile across the room. A 90-degree layout will minimize the effects of wear.

Carpet tile is made in different dye lots, but unlike other tile, it's not easy to mix the dye lots in a random pattern. Lay different dye lots in different rooms when possible.

Arrows on the back of carpet tile indicate the direction of the pile.

LAYING THE TILE

1 Snap and square chalk lines to locate the center of the room and divide it into quadrants (see *pages 160–161)*. Dry-lay a row of tile on both axes and adjust the rows to create even borders at each end. Peel the backing off the first tile and lay it square on the chalk lines. For most installations, you can set the tiles in concentric squares around the center, or in quadrants.

2 As you lay the succeeding tiles, always set them with the leading edges against the previous tiles and the arrows consistent with the pattern you have chosen. Lay the tile in place, don't slide it. Use a stairstep pattern when possible so you have two edges to set the next tile against. Roll the tile to adhere it soundly.

CUTTING CARPET TILE

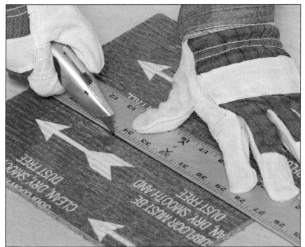

Use the same techniques to line up carpet tile for cuts as you would for ceramic and resilient tile (see *pages 168–169)*, but set the tile to be cut face down. Mark the cut line on the back of the tile. Set a steel straightedge along the marker line and make several light passes along it with a sharp utility knife. Once you have cut through the backing, bend the tile and cut through the pile.

CARPET TILE TIPS

Self-stick carpet tile is fairly thin and readily shows subfloor imperfections. Make sure you prepare a smooth surface before laying it.

If you're installing dry-back tile, apply the adhesive with a paint roller and let it become tacky. Most mastics allow plenty of working time so you can reposition the tile if necessary without having to rush.

When working with either kind of tile, push the edges tightly against each other, but don't crush them together. The best way to get a good joint is to start with the tile slightly raised at one edge with the opposite edge pushed against a tile already in place. Make sure the corners of the new tile are lined up with the corners of the others, then lower it into place.

INSTALLING LAMINATE TILE

Laminate tiles snap together, but each brand uses a different method. Some laminates come with simple tongues and grooves. Others have tongue-and-groove edges modified with a locking bead along the tongue. Still other types use metal locking strips on the edges of the tile.

The most common way to set the tiles in place is the tilt-and-engage method shown on these pages. The easiest way to start the first rows is by pulling the tile toward you. Once you have locked the edge row in place, move it away from the wall and assemble the next two rows by pulling the tile together. With three rows pushed against the wall, you'll have enough leverage to complete the floor by pushing the tiles together.

Some products are not recommended for bathrooms. Others have joints that can be sealed with glue to make them water-resistant.

LAYING THE TILE

1 If you're tiling over a concrete slab, cover it with 6-mil sheet polyethylene waterproofing membrane. Then roll out the underlayment, following the manufacturer's directions for bonding the seams. If your plans call for laminate baseboards or you're tiling a bathroom or kitchen, extend the underlayment 2 to 3 inches up the wall and tape the seams with waterproof tape.

2 Snap and square chalk lines on the underlayment between the midpoints of opposite walls (see *page 160*). Dry-lay the tile in both directions and adjust the rows until you have edge tiles that are at least a half-tile wide and equal at each end.

3 Measure the width of the edge tiles and cut them with a circular saw (with the finished side of the tile facing downward) or tablesaw (with the finished side up).

4 Set the edge row against the wall, following the manufacturer's assembly directions. Most tiles lock together by holding the tile at an angle, inserting the tongue of one tile into the groove of another, and pushing down.

5 Slide the assembled edge row 2 to 3 feet away from the wall. Lock the second row of tiles to the first, using the same technique, tilting the tiles and pulling the tongue into the groove. Prop the tile on a piece of scrap to make the process easier.

6 Depending on the manufacturer's instructions, you can either pull each tile toward you and into the adjacent tiles or assemble an entire row separately and lock it to the previous row. Regardless of the method, you should lower the tile until you feel or hear it snap into place.

7 When you have assembled the first three rows, slide them toward the starting wall, leaving enough space for the thickness of the spacers. Insert the spacers against the wall and snug the rows against them. Continue assembling the tile across the remainder of the room.

INSTALLING TRANSITIONS

Baseboards and transitions don't just finish out a floor. They join different flooring material, often in doorways. They hide the cut edges of the tile you've laid, serve as visual accents, signify the change from one room and one flooring material to another, and help prevent tripping and falling by smoothing the transition between different materials.

Baseboards are an important stylistic element, so you should choose the molding carefully. Many homes have standard streamline—or ranch—molding, which is inexpensive but may not be the best style for your interior design. You can reinstall your existing molding, but you might want to consider alternatives. A surprising variety of baseboard styles is available in milled stock at your local home center. Select a molding pattern that fits the style and the function of the room. A standard streamline molding might be the right thing for a children's playroom, while a larger, more elaborate design would be more attractive in the dining room. You can combine moldings to create a custom look too.

If you plan to paint the baseboard, buy paintable pine or medium-density fiberboard (MDF) moldings. But if the molding will be stained or clear-finished, select a hardwood molding. Try to match wood species and finish if there's existing woodwork in the room.

INSTALLING TRANSITIONS

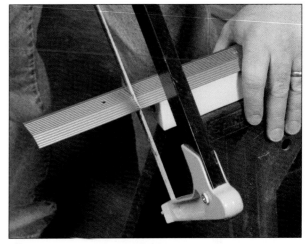

1️⃣ Measure the width of the doorway and subtract $\frac{1}{16}$ inch so the transition will slide into the opening easily. Cut a piece of thin scrap to this length and test-fit it in the opening.

2️⃣ Adjust the measurement, if necessary, and mark your transition stock for cutting at this length. Clamp the transition to a work surface and cut it. Use a hacksaw with a fine-tooth blade to cut metal stock, applying moderate clamping pressure to avoid bending it. Use a toolbox handsaw or tablesaw to cut a wood threshold.

3️⃣ Slide the transition into the opening and fasten it with ringshank nails, brass wood screws, or the fasteners recommended by the manufacturer. If you're installing a wood threshold, predrill it and the subfloor at the same time. Then drive screws to fasten it to the floor.

TYPICAL TRANSITIONS

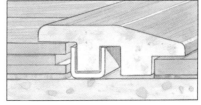

A reducer strip eases the transition from a thicker to thinner floor, from wood to vinyl, for example.

Install a universal threshold when wood flooring butts against a carpeted floor.

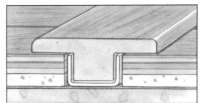

T-molding provides a transition between flooring material of the same height.

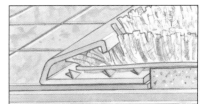

Carpet edging has a lip that locks into the fabric. After the carpet is inserted, fold the lip down.

CHAPTER HIGHLIGHTS

This chapter illustrates techniques and

tips you will need to lay tile on

kitchen and bathroom walls. It also

covers countertops and projects

such as chair rail, murals, and

window rosettes that enhance

the style of a room.

TILING WALLS AND COUNTERTOPS

Most of the techniques for installing tile on walls and countertops are the same as those used on floors, but floor tiles must have qualities that those used on walls and counters don't need.

The chief concern when buying floor tiles is performance: how well the tile stands up to wear and tear, heavy loads, and potential slippery conditions. Walls and countertops don't have those requirements, so you can choose from many more types of tile.

And while even the most decorative floors usually serve only as a background for the design elements in a room, walls and countertops are design elements in their own right. You can focus your attention on color, texture, pattern, and variety when you select tile for these projects.

Most standard wall tiles come in $4\frac{1}{4}$-inch squares, both lugged (prespaced for about $\frac{1}{16}$-inch joints) and unlugged. Standard wall tiles are often soft enough so you can cut them with hand tools; this softness makes them unsuitable for floors. All floor tiles, however, can be put on walls. The only requirement is a solid substrate so the wall won't crack in tile or grout lines. Glazed vitreous tiles are the most popular countertop tiles—choose light colors if hiding scratches is a priority.

TILING A WALL

Tiling a wall is much easier than tiling a floor in many ways, mostly because you're working upright, and that takes less energy than moving around on your knees. Walls, however, offer some unique problems. The most obvious is that gravity wants to slide the tiles down the wall. Also, wall corners are often out of plumb.

You can overcome gravity with organic mastic–tiles stick to it almost immediately. Even though it's not as strong as thinset, mastic is effective on walls that won't get wet.

Use spacers, nails, or tape–or a combination of the three–to space wall tiles in thinset. Plan ahead so you're not surprised by out-of-plumb corners. Skim-coat thinset to level the walls. Then use wide tiles on inside corners and overlapped bullnose tiles on outside corners.

INSTALLING THE TILE

1 Because most floors will not be exactly level, you will probably have a tapered row of tiles at the top and bottom. To keep the rows level across the wall, tack a 1× batten along the bottom of the wall on the plane where your first full tiles will be laid. The batten will also prevent the tiles from sliding down the wall. If your layout calls for a coved tile base, install it first, leveling it with plastic wedges. Then tile up the wall.

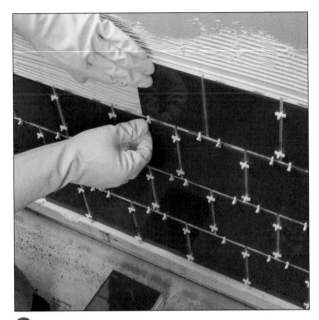

2 Spread and comb mortar on the wall in sections, pushing each tile into the mortar. Insert spacers as you go, sliding the tile against the spacers. If you insert the spacers as shown above, they will be easier to remove. When you've laid the field tile and the mortar is dry, remove the batten, then cut and install the edge tiles.

3 Even with a batten and spacers, you may have to take extra steps to keep the tile on the wall while the adhesive cures. To ensure that your tiles stay put, drive nails halfway into the wall, and tape the tiles with masking tape.

4 Before the mortar cures, drag a spacer in the joints to clean out the excess. If you find any hardened mortar after it cures, remove it with a grout knife and clean any excess from the tile surface. Mix enough grout to cover a section, then force it into the joints with a grout float, keeping the float at a 45-degree angle. Work the float diagonally in both directions to fill the joints.

TILING OUT-OF-PLUMB WALLS

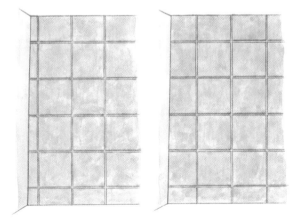

Walls are seldom perfectly plumb, but you may be able to improve that condition with a skim coat of thinset (see page 164). If abutting walls are out of plumb, narrow tiles in the corner will make it more noticeable. Lay out the tiles to place nearly full-sized tiles in the corners to minimize the effect.

TILING A COUNTERTOP AND BACKSPLASH

Tiling a countertop is a little like tiling a floor and wall in the same project–except you're working at about waist height. A tile countertop needs a strong plywood base supported by 1× framing, topped with a waterproofing membrane and backerboard. Backerboard is optional (but preferred) for the backsplash.

Tile the countertop first, using latex- or acrylic-modified adhesives and grout. Before you tile the backsplash, set the countertop edge tiles and let the mortar cure. Or, you can lay the backsplash tiles before the countertop edge. Either way, you won't disturb the edge tiles when you lean over them to work. Tile the backsplash from bottom to top, hiding any cut edges under the cabinets. Design the layout so you don't have to cut decorative molding to fit electrical outlets. Seal the grout joints to protect them from staining.

INSTALLING THE TILE

1 Using the tile dimensions as a guide, snap as many layout lines on the countertop and backsplash as you need to help you keep the tiles straight. Be sure to snap a line for the edge tiles, both along the front of the countertop and around the border of the sink.

2 Spread thinset on the countertop in sections between your layout lines. Lay all of the field tile, then clean excess mortar from the grout lines by dragging a spacer through the joints. Let the thinset cure overnight.

3 Cut and install the tile that borders the sink. Dry-fit the corners to make sure the grout line will be the same width as the others. Spread thinset on the backerboard and back-butter the border tiles.

4 Back-butter the bullnose tile and lay it on the front edge of the countertop. Tack a wood batten along the edge to aid in alignment. Let the mortar cure, then remove the batten. Back-butter the front edge tiles and install them. Tape the tiles in place.

5 Grout the tile in sections with a grout float (see *page 71*), and remove excess grout with the float. When the grout sets up slightly, clean each section. Then smooth the joints with a wrung-out sponge. Repeat the cleaning and wipe off the haze.

EDGING WITH V-CAP OR WOOD

To trim the counter with V-cap edging, first trowel thinset on the top of the countertop edge. Then back-butter the inside bottom edge of the V-cap and press it into the mortar. You may need to center the V-cap between the grout joints. This will make the grout joints slightly wider, but not enough to be apparent.

To install a wood edge *(above, right),* wait for the mortar to set, then fasten the edging to the base with 6d finish nails.

TILING A BACKSPLASH

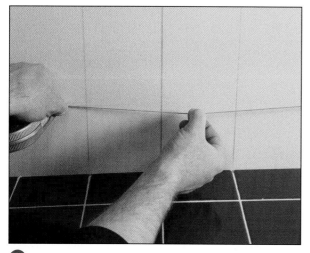

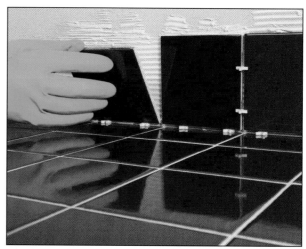

1 Hold a tile against the backsplash in line with the countertop grout lines, resting the tile on spacers. Mark the edge of the tile, remove it, and snap level and square layout lines across the wall.

2 Trowel mortar on the backsplash and set the bottom row of tiles, inserting spacers along the bottom edge. Make sure the top edge is lined up with your layout lines. Set the remaining tiles, cleaning the grout lines with a spacer as you go. Let the mortar cure.

OFFSETTING THE GROUT LINES

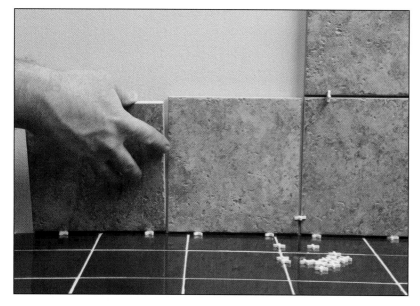

You can create an interesting design by covering the countertop and backsplash with different tiles. Backsplash tiles that are not the same size as those on the countertop will create offset grout lines. Plan the layout carefully with dry-laid tiles. Once you have established the layout, mark the backsplash and snap layout lines. Install the tiles with the same techniques as you would other backsplash tile.

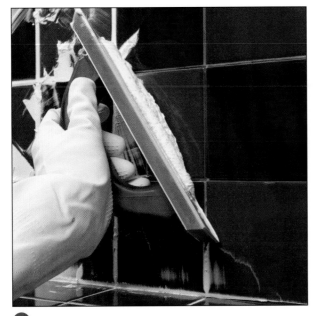

3 Remove the spacers and grout the tiles with a grout float. Do not grout the joint where the backsplash and countertop meet. Work the float in both directions to fill the joints.

4 Let the grout set until you can't pull it out of the joint with a slightly damp sponge. Then scrape the excess grout off the tile surface with the grout float. Clean the excess from the surface and smooth the joints with a damp sponge. Caulk the joint along the bottom of the backsplash.

LAYING A DIAGONAL BACKSPLASH

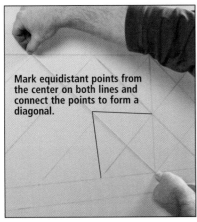

Mark equidistant points from the center on both lines and connect the points to form a diagonal.

1 At the horizontal and vertical midpoints of the backsplash, snap perpendicular chalk lines. From their intersection, measure an equal distance on each line. Connect these points to form a diagonal and snap lines parallel to it.

2 Divide the backsplash into four sections and trowel on thinset in one section. Set the tiles and clean the joints in that quadrant, then in the remaining quadrants. Let the mortar cure, then cut and install the edge tile.

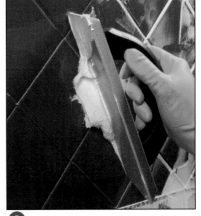

3 Force grout into the joints with the grout float. Let the grout set up slightly and remove the excess with the float. Clean the surface at least twice with a damp sponge and clean water. Wipe the haze from the surface with a clean rag.

TILING A WALL MURAL

A tiled mural can bring an exciting design element not just to a kitchen backsplash, but to any wall. Murals, in which a single image extends over a number of tiles, come in a wide array of designs, many of them available at your home center or tile retailer. Search the Internet for "tile murals" if you're looking for a one-of-a-kind design. Or make your own mural with special ceramic water-based paints you can cure in your kitchen oven. Also, many ceramics shops will provide you with the tile, paints, and glazes, then fire your artwork when you are done.

No matter where you install a mural, planning a precise layout is the key. If you're setting a freestanding mural on an untiled wall,

layout is relatively easy. Dry-lay the mural on a flat surface with spacers, measure the layout accurately, then transfer the measurements to the wall, keeping the perimeter plumb and level with a carpenter's level.

To incorporate a mural into a tiled wall, lay out the mural on a large piece of cardboard and cut the cardboard to its exact dimensions. Then use the cardboard to lay out the wall tile, adjusting the position of the mural so it creates the least number of cut wall tiles. It's usually better to set full tiles next to the mural, leaving cut tiles at the edges of the wall. Snap layout lines on the wall and install the mural first so you won't have to worry about the mural not fitting after tiling the wall.

INSTALLING THE TILE

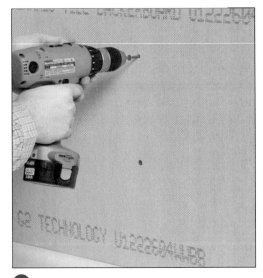

1 Prepare the wall. If you're not tiling the rest of the wall, you probably won't need backerboard. If the mural will be on a wall that might get wet, cut backerboard to fit the wall and fasten it with backerboard screws.

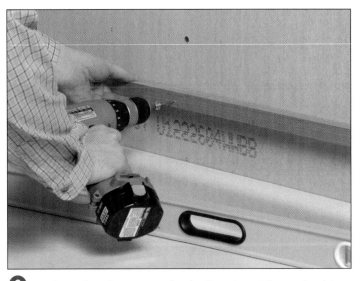

2 Snap layout lines that correspond to the dimensions of the mural and the individual tiles. If your mural will be framed with wood, fasten the bottom piece along your layout line. If you will tile the rest of the wall, install decorative border tiles (see *pages 24–25*). If you won't have a border, tack a batten along your layout line to help keep the tiles straight and level.

3 Trowel thinset onto the wall, then set the bottom tiles with a slight twist. Set the remaining tiles, keeping the joints tight as you adjust the tiles to keep them lined up. It's more important that the pattern have an aesthetically pleasing look than that the tiles are set right on the lines.

4 When the mural is complete, stand back a few feet and make sure the pattern is lined up and centered in the area. Grout the tile when the mortar cures, and seal the grout if necessary.

TILING A CHAIR RAIL

Installing a tiled chair rail adds architectural interest to a wall; it's not only decorative, it helps break up the otherwise bare expanse of a wall. You can start and finish the project in a weekend afternoon.

Choose a tile for your chair rail that complements the overall character of your room. Ask your retailer for help if you're having trouble choosing the right tile. Raised listellos (see *page 27)* are commonly used, but you can also use embossed flat tiles to create a stand-alone border. You won't need to worry about the appearance of cut listellos at the corners–they won't be apparent. Even so, it's best to start a border with full tiles in the most visible corners, leaving cut tiles where they won't be so noticeable.

Roughen the paint on the wall under the tile so the adhesive will stick to it. If you're installing the rail on an unpainted wall, lay the tile first, then paint the wall.

INSTALLING THE TILE

1 Measure 36 inches from the floor and mark the wall. This is your layout line for the top edge of the chair rail tile. Extend this mark along the wall with a carpenter's level. If the wall is painted, roughen the paint below the layout line with 80-grit sandpaper.

2 Make a 45-degree jig from a piece of 2× scrap. Clamp the jig on the bed of a wet saw and miter two pieces of chair rail. These corner pieces should be at least 6 inches long.

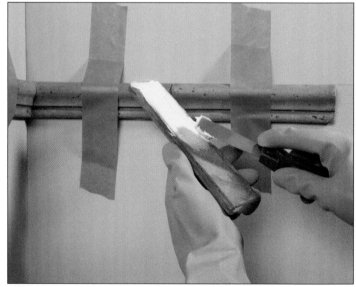

3 Back-butter each tile with latex thinset. Push the tile onto the wall aligned exactly with the layout line. Clean off excess mortar immediately. Support the tile with painter's tape that won't pull the paint off the wall.

TILING WINDOW ROSETTES

Ceramic tile window rosettes, a common feature in early 20th-century homes, gradually lost favor as lower costs became a more important consideration in home construction. But now, you can add this decorative feature to your window trim at modest cost and with little effort. However, rosettes are not well-suited to windows that have coved trim.

Make sure the corner inserts fit tightly and that their top and bottom edges are parallel to the top window casing. Finish the corner inserts to match the wood. If your window trim is painted, you may have to repaint if the fresh paint on the rosette frames doesn't match the old paint on the window trim.

INSTALLING THE TILE

1 Mark the corner of the casing with a combination square. Cut the corners out with a backsaw. If the cut corner holds a fastener, you'll have to pry it away and fasten the top casing by driving 6d finishing nails into the wall framing.

2 Cut lauan plywood to fit into the corners you have cut away. Using mitered cove molding, construct a four-sided frame. Fasten the plywood to the back of the molding frame with brads.

3 Predrill the plywood before you attach the frames to the recess in the casing. Then drive three 1⅝-inch drywall screws through the plywood and drywall and into the wall framing behind it.

4 Apply a ¼-inch bead of silicone adhesive to the back of the tile, center the tile, then press it into the frame.

Tiling a fireplace can enhance the character of a room. When planning your design, restrain your enthusiasm a bit; too much enhancement can cause the fireplace to stand out and separate itself from the room's overall design scheme. The fireplace should serve as an accent in the room, not an element that overwhelms everything around it.

Ceramic tiles can take the heat generated by a fireplace, but most mortars will not. Heat-resistant thinset rated for temperatures of up to 400 degrees is available. Heat-resistant cement-based mortar works well on masonry surfaces.

When planning the substrate, you have a number of options. You can tile over existing tile or brick, spreading thinset as a base for the new tile and leveling it with a 2×4 screed. If the existing surface is drywall or plaster, or if it is in poor condition, skim-coat it with thinset and attach backerboard. Backerboard is required when covering a metal surround and when tiling a hearth, which must withstand the shock of dropped logs as well as the heat.

Tile is not indestructible. Ceramic and porcelain floor tiles are tough and should stand up to dropped firewood, but saltillo and marble will crack. Marble also stains easily; sealing it will minimize—but not eliminate—black marks from soot or thrown embers.

When you decide to tile a fireplace surround, experiment with different layouts on paper. Draw your fireplace to scale on ¼-inch graph paper, and use tracing paper to try out different tile designs. That way, you can use a larger tile if a small style results in narrow cut edges. Consider tiling the inside front edge of the firebox too. Leaving it untiled might make your installation look incomplete. Use bullnose if it's available; if it's not, cut field tile and round the edges.

INSTALLING THE TILE

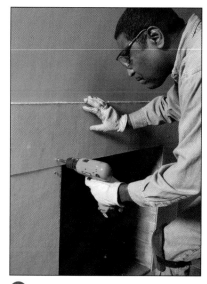  

1 Measure the dimensions of the surfaces around the fireplace opening and cut backerboard to fit. Install the backerboard with heat-resistant thinset and self-tapping masonry screws. Tape and finish any joints in the backerboard using fiberglass mesh tape and thinset.

2 Dry-lay your tiles on the floor in front of the fireplace, keeping the arrangement to the same dimensions as the backerboard. Place inset tiles on the field tiles and mark their outlines. Cut the field tile and test-fit all the tiles. You may have to trim the outside edges of the field tiles to make the insets fit and still leave enough room for grout joints. Number the tiles to indicate their placement.

3 Set the field tiles in heat-resistant thinset and let the mortar set up. Then install the inset tiles, taping them in place until the mortar sets up. You can finish the inside edge of the fireplace opening with trim tile, bullnose, or cut field tile, rounding the cut edges with a masonry stone after the mortar cures.

TILING THE INSIDE OF THE OPENING

Whatever kind of tile you use to finish the inside edge of the opening, support it with a 2x4 until the mortar has cured. Support the 2x4 with legs slightly longer than the distance to the floor. Force the legs in just hard enough to keep the 2x4 in place without compressing the tiles into the mortar.

FIREPLACE CODES

Before you start, check your local building codes. Some areas consider a tiled fireplace as new construction, and you may need a permit to do the work.

Codes are detailed and specific about anything that involves fire. You may have to keep combustible materials, such as the mantel shelf, a specified distance from the firebox. You may also need to schedule an inspection of your fireplace to make sure the damper and chimney are in good working condition. If they're not, the addition of a new chimney liner may satisfy the inspectors.

Tiling a Wood Stove Enclosure

A wood-burning stove or freestanding fireplace can make a room seem warm even when there's no fire inside.

The primary decision to make is where to put the stove and where to route the chimney—through a wall or through the ceiling. Both methods would comply with building codes in most areas (but be sure to check), so this decision will probably depend more on the location of the stove or fireplace. Another factor is whether you want to add the fixture to a room without making major changes or remodel the room to accommodate it. Setting the stove or fireplace in a corner is an easy way to incorporate it into an existing room. A three-sided enclosure is one way to alter a room for the fireplace or stove.

All codes require air space between the tile and a combustible surface. Hat channel, light-gauge sheet-metal track, is the ideal material for this purpose (don't use wooden 2×4s).

Make a sketch of your proposed stove location and the tile pattern you want to use. Consider the stove and the tiled area as one design element rather than viewing the tiled surfaces as just a backdrop for the stove.

Make the space large enough (54 inches or more) to fit the scale of the room and provide the clearance from surfaces recommended by the stove or fireplace manufacturer. Make sure the floor can support the combined weight of the stove and the tile base. Hire an architect or consulting engineer if you're not sure.

INSTALLING THE TILE

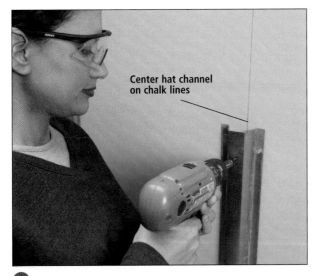

Center hat channel on chalk lines

1 Locate the wall studs and mark their centers on the wall. Set a carpenter's level on the marks, plumb the level, and extend the marks down the wall. Cut sections of hat channel to the height of the heat shield and fasten it to the studs with 2½-inch screws.

2 Cut two sheets of backerboard to the dimensions of the heat shield and mark one with lines that correspond to the centers of the hat channel. Assemble the sheets with a thin coat of heat-resistant thinset. Hold the assembly against the hat channel with the edges flush and the lines centered on the hat channel. Fasten the shield every 4 inches with 1½-inch, self-tapping, sheet metal screws. Tape and finish any joints.

3 If you're installing a tiled base for the stove (see *right*), set it in place before you lay the wall tile. Or, tack a batten of ¼-inch plywood along the bottom of the wall to keep the tiles off the floor. Trowel heat-resistant thinset onto the backerboard, then lay the bottom row of tiles. Set the remaining rows with spacers, and line them up with a carpenter's level. Let the mortar cure for 24 hours, grout the tiles, remove the batten, then caulk the joint at the floor.

TILING A STOVE BASE

If you're installing a tiled stove base, assemble and install it before installing the heat shield. Build the base from ¾-inch plywood and 1× or 2× edging—cut to the same dimensions as an even multiple of your tiles so you won't have to cut edge tiles. Use the techniques shown for tiling a countertop (see *pages 72–75*). Back-butter bullnose or trim tiles on the sides of the platform. Grout the joints.

CHAPTER HIGHLIGHTS

This chapter illustrates the techniques used to install tile in the most common bathroom locations—a tub or shower surround, a custom shower pan, and a vanity. It also provides tips for designing these applications.

TILING TUBS, SHOWERS, & VANITIES

Ceramic tile is durable, water-resistant, and easy to clean: the ideal material to withstand the challenges of daily bathroom use. And tile allows you to create a variety of styles and looks that can make a distinctive room.

Laying out a tile installation in a bathroom can at first appear complicated, especially if you are creating a design ensemble—tiling the floor, tub surround, vanity, and walls. If you take the project one step (or one surface) at a time, however, and plan your layout on graph paper, it will easily fall into place.

Start by looking for the largest open area on the walls and floor (remember that you will remove the fixtures before tiling). Mark the center of these areas on your plan and use the dimensions of your tile to predict where the grout lines will fall. Adjust the joints on the wall to correspond to those in the floor—it's easier to do this and less noticeable if you use small tiles. Then decide on a pattern for the vanity tiles and the tub or shower surround.

If you plan to mix different kinds of ceramic tile, be sure they're exactly the same thickness, length, and width. Even a difference of ½₂ inch will make a noticeable difference on the surface and can cause grout lines to be obviously misaligned.

If you're tiling the bathroom floor, remove the toilet and sink and use the same techniques you would use on a kitchen floor (see *pages 46–49*).

Tiling a Shower Enclosure or Tub Surround

Tub and shower surrounds will get wet, so installing tile in these locations requires some extra preparation steps not required in dry installations.

First, you have to protect the framing from water by covering it with 15-pound felt paper or 4-mil polyethylene sheets. This waterproofing membrane goes directly on the studs, and has overlapping seams sealed with asphalt roofing mastic. Cement backerboard over the membrane provides a stable base for tile.

Tile should extend about 12 inches above the tub edge or at least 6 inches above the showerhead in a shower enclosure. You can tile the ceiling if you want to, but aligning the grout joints with those in the wall will be difficult if the walls are not square—and they usually aren't. A diagonal tile pattern on the ceiling can help you avoid this problem.

A bathtub project is more complicated because you have to coat the front face of the tub flange with asphalt mastic and seal the waterproofing membrane to it. This is the place where most tub and shower surrounds leak; water that gets into this joint will migrate up the flange, down the studs, then into the floor.

If the tub is level, you can set the bottom row of the surround in full tiles. If the tub isn't level, make the bottom row about three-fourths of a tile high and tack a level batten at this height. The larger the tile, the less awkward a tapered bottom row will look.

If your shower has an outside window, consider replacing it with glass block. You'll gain privacy without sacrificing light, and you'll greatly eliminate the possibility that moisture will get behind the tile from the edges of the window.

INSTALLING BACKERBOARD

1 Spread a coat of asphalt mastic on the front of the tub flange. Cut felt paper long enough to cover the entire surface in a single run. Spread asphalt mastic on the bottom half of the studs. Then set the felt paper on the edge of the tub and press it into the mastic on the tub flange and the mastic on the studs. Staple the paper, warming it with a hair dryer and smoothing it as you go. Overlap upper pieces over lower ones and seal the overlaps with mastic.

2 Cut and fasten backerboard to the studs with backerboard screws, centering the edges of the sheets on the studs and setting the backerboard on ¼-inch spacers. Reinforce the corners with fiberglass mesh tape. Skim-coat all the joints with thinset, let it dry, then sand it smooth.

3 Remove the spacers and caulk the gap at the bottom of the backerboard with clear or white silicone caulk. Caulk seals the gap between the tub and backerboard and allows the materials to expand and contract at different rates without cracking the joints.

SETTING THE TILE

1 To keep the tiles level, tack a 1× batten to the backerboard one full tile width above the tub if the tub is level. If not, place the batten three-fourths of a tile width above the edge. Cover the tub with heavy paper to protect it from dropped tiles and grit on your shoes.

2 Using the dimensions of your tile, locate a point where a horizontal and vertical grout line will intersect. Hold a 4-foot level on both planes and mark layout lines, snapping chalk lines to extend them to the walls and ceiling. Then snap layout grids equal to the width of the tiles and grout.

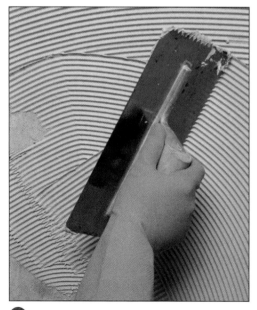

3 Mix as much of the adhesive as you can use before it sets up, and trowel it onto the backerboard in sections.

4 Set the field tiles on the back wall first, but don't set the edge tiles or tiles around fixtures. When the back wall is done, start the side walls with full tiles along the front edge. This will put the cut tiles in the back corner, where they will be less noticeable.

5 After the adhesive has dried overnight, cut and set the edge tiles and remove excess adhesive from the joints. Then mark the tiles to fit around the showerhead and faucet, leaving a ¼-inch gap around the fixtures. Seal that gap with silicone caulk and let the adhesive cure.

6 When the adhesive is dry, clean excess mortar from the surface and joints. Mix grout and apply it with a grout float, forcing it into the joints in both directions. Take up the excess with the float, and let the grout set up until a damp sponge won't lift it out of the joints.

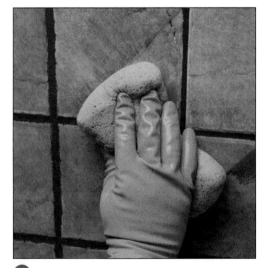

7 Dampen a sponge, wring it out thoroughly, and clean the surface twice, smoothing the joints. Scrub off the haze with a clean rag.

HANGING SURFACE FIXTURES

When you set the wall tiles in a shower surround, leave a space for surface-mounted accessories, such as soap dishes and shelves. Cut the tile to leave an opening the size of the accessory. Spread mortar on the wall and back-butter the accessory. Center it, tape it in place until the mortar dries, then caulk the joint.

TILING A CUSTOM SHOWER PAN

Prefabricated shower units are great for some installations, but if you need shower space customized to fit your space, you'll have to install a mortared shower pan. This installation is not quite as simple as a thinset project, but with patience and careful attention, laying a mortared shower pan is within the ability of most homeowners.

When you're selecting tile, think small—smaller tiles will conform to the slope of a shower floor better than larger tiles. Square 4-inch tile will usually work fine, but 12-inch tiles could cause a lot more work.

Start your project by making sure your floor can support the weight of the shower. Consult with a contractor if you have any doubts. Then install the drain lines and build the frame. Coat the inside of the drain with PVC primer and cement and twist the drain onto the waste line. Then insert the drain bolts into the lower drain plate, and mix and apply the mortar (called deck mud in the trade). The consistency of deck

mud is like a sandy clay, just wet enough to clump together. You'll know it's right if it holds its shape when you squeeze it.

Float the bed in two steps: float the sloped subbase over which you will install the membrane, and float another sloped mortar bed over that. Both layers must drop ¼ inch for every linear foot of floor surface.

Use chlorinated polyethylene (CPE) or polyvinyl chloride (PVC) membrane for the pan. Both are tough, flexible plastics that resist punctures. PVC is easier to find in some areas. If you have trouble keeping the membrane flat, you can trowel on a thin coat of asphalt mastic to adhere it. If the enclosure is larger than the membrane, join an additional section by solvent welding. Use the solvent recommended by the membrane manufacturer, and follow the solvent instructions. You will also solvent-weld the membrane in the corners.

If you puncture the membrane, cut a 2-inch patch and solvent-weld it over the puncture.

BUILDING THE BASE

Curb

1 Make sure your floor can support the weight of the shower unit, and shore it up, if necessary. Strip off any finished flooring to the underlayment, replacing the subfloor with ¾-inch exterior plywood if it's not in good repair. Erect and brace the walls with studs on 16-inch centers. Cut pressure-treated bottom plates and fasten them to the floor with 3-inch decking screws. Tie the top corners of the walls together. Toe-nail 2×10 blocking between the studs to support the membrane. Assemble the curb from three pressure-treated 2×4s. Tack ¾-inch guides around the perimeter (not necessary for stalls larger than 4 feet on both sides). Cut a hole in the center of the floor and fit the lower drain plate.

2 Cut 15-pound felt to fit the floor and staple it to the floor. Then cut a sheet of metal lath and set it in place. Staple the metal lath to the floor, flattening any bumps that could weaken the subbase. Then use aviation snips to cut out a circle about an inch wider than the drain.

3 In a wheelbarrow (not a bucket), mix the deck mud from bagged sand mix (4 parts sand, 1 part portland cement) and latex additive (not water). Dump the mortar onto the floor, spreading it with a wood float and sloping it from the top of the ¾-inch guides (or the bottom wall plate on larger stalls) to the top of the drain flange. Compact the mortar into an even, level surface and let it dry overnight.

4 Set the membrane on the floor of the stall and unroll it from front to back, covering the front of the curb. Working from the drain outward, smooth out air bubbles. Then staple the top 1 inch of the membrane to the 2×10 blocking. Fold and solvent-weld the corners rather than cutting them to ensure it remains watertight.

LAYING THE TILE

1 Expose each drain bolt by pressing the membrane down until the bolt profile shows through the membrane. Cut a ⅜-inch X in the membrane over the bolts—just enough to allow you to push the membrane over the bolt head. Then unscrew the bolts so you can fasten the upper drain plate.

2 Set the upper drain plate with the holes directly on the X-cuts in the membrane. Don't seal the bottom of this plate—it will clog the weep holes. Insert the bolts in the holes, turn the plate to lock it, and tighten the bolts evenly with a wrench. Using a long sharp knife, carefully cut away the membrane in the drain hole. (Don't use a utility knife. Its blade is not long enough to make a clean cut.) Then check for leaks by filling the pan with water and letting it stand overnight.

3 Wrap the threads of the strainer with plumber's tape and screw the strainer into the flange. To protect the strainer and drain from stray mortar and thinset, apply two layers of crisscrossed masking tape. Cut the tape flush around the edge of the strainer.

4 Insulate any exterior walls with fiberglass batts. Then cut sheets of 4-mil polyethylene waterproofing membrane long enough to hang from the top of the walls to 3 or 4 inches below the top edge of the pan membrane. Using only four or five staples on each stud, attach the poly, but don't put staples through the pan membrane lower than 1 inch from its top edge.

5 Clean any grit from the membrane with a damp cloth and, for extra protection from punctures, cover the liner with a drop cloth. Cut backerboard to fit the walls and set it on ½-inch shims. Fasten the backerboard to the studs with backerboard screws (see *pages 156-159)*; keep the screws within the top 1 inch of the pan membrane. Remove the shims and caulk the gap at the bottom of the backerboard with silicone. Tape and mud the seams with latex-modified thinset.

6 Mark the upper edge of the pan on the walls, tying the marks together with a chalk line. Mix up another batch of dry mortar. Spread the mortar from the drain to about halfway to your marks, keeping the slope at about one-third of a bubble on a level. This is the first course of deck mud. Lay metal lath over the first course, then pack and level a top layer of mud, starting at the marks on the wall and working toward the drain. Work in sections, sloping the floor toward the drain. Bend lath to fit the curb and pack it also, slanting the top inward.

7 When the deck mud has dried, scrape off any high spots with a steel trowel, then spread and comb latex-modified thinset. Press the tiles firmly into the mortar. Line up all the edges with a 2-foot straightedge and let the mortar cure overnight. Grout the tiles with latex-modified grout, cleaning off the excess and scrubbing off the grout haze.

CHECK FOR LEAKS

Check the membrane for leaks by plugging the drain with an expandable stopper and filling the pan with water to within 1 inch of the top. Mark the water level on the side of the pan, and let it sit for 24 hours. If the level is still on the mark, the pan is watertight. If the water is below the mark, there is a leak, and you'll have to find it. If the floor outside the perimeter is wet, the leak is on the side. Solvent-weld a patch on the hole and retest the pan.

If the water has drained out completely, tighten the drain bolts a little. If the flange has cut the membrane, take up the drain plate, let the membrane dry, and solvent-weld a patch at least 2 inches larger than the puncture.

TILING A VANITY

Tiling the vanity is a great way to give a bathroom a new look without a complete remodel. You don't even have to buy a new vanity, but you will have to take off the old countertop. You'll also probably have to strengthen the frame of the vanity with 1× supports, then build a new, stronger base from ¾-inch exterior plywood (see *pages 154–155).* It's also a good idea to treat the vanity countertop as a kitchen counter, installing a waterproofing membrane and backerboard on the plywood.

Choose tile that will complement the style of the bathroom. When picking tile color, consider any new paint color you plan to use. Glazed tile ⅜ to ½ inch thick is the best choice. When you decide on a style, buy all the tile you need–the vanity tile, the backsplash tile, the wall tile, and bullnose trim–from the same lot. That way, your tiles will have a more consistent color throughout the entire project. Make sure the cartons have the same lot number.

Your sink choice is important too. You can reuse the old sink, but you'll probably want a new sink as part of your new design. Purchase a sink to go with the color and glaze of the tile–vitreous china and enameled cast iron are good choices. Self-rimming sinks are easy to install, and the rim covers the cut edges of the tile.

INSTALLING THE TILE

1 You can construct a tile base on a new or existing vanity. For added strength, glue and screw bracing inside the cabinet, then install a ¾-inch exterior-plywood base with a 1-inch overhang. Staple plastic sheeting to the plywood and install ½-inch backerboard.

2 Mark the cut line of the sink using the manufacturer's template. If a template isn't included, center the sink upside down on the surface and outline its shape. Draw a second line 1 inch inside the first line and drill a starter hole. Cut along the inside line with a jigsaw.

3 Lay out and space the tiles in a dry run. Adjust the tile to minimize cutting. Mark the edges of the tiles when you're satisfied with the layout, then snap parallel chalk lines on the marks.

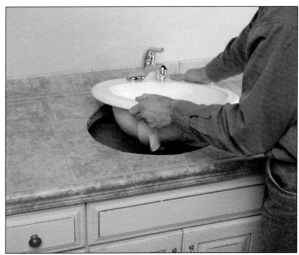

4 Comb thinset onto the backerboard. Set the tiles in the mortar with a slight twist and level them with a beater block (see *page 51*). The tiles around the sink hole don't have to run perfectly around the edge of the hole—but don't extend them beyond the edge. Keep the tiles in line using a carpenter's level. Let the mortar cure, then grout the tiles (see *pages 170–171*).

5 When the grout has cured, run a bead of silicone caulk around the edge of the sink hole and lower the sink in place. Ask someone to help support the sink from below. Install and tighten any mounting clips and hook up the plumbing. Run another bead of caulk around the edge of the sink and smooth it with a wet finger.

CHAPTER HIGHLIGHTS

This chapter shows how tile can transform common objects—a table, address numerals, stepping-stones, a precast concrete bench, and a birdbath—into attractive and useful decorative items for inside and outside your home.

TILING DECORATIVE ACCENTS

If you're looking for a project the whole family can enjoy, or one that will give you a chance to easily express your creativity, you'll probably find it in this chapter.

Some of these projects use full tiles and call for the same techniques as tiling a floor or wall–just on a smaller scale. These are great projects to try if you want to practice working with tile before you tackle a larger project in your home.

Other projects make use of pieces of broken tiles laid as a mosaic design. Mosaics can be made of almost anything: tiles left over from tiling a wall or floor, old plates and china, glass marbles, even old glassware. You should keep the thickness of the material fairly consistent throughout the project. To make the small pieces, wrap up one item at a time in an old towel or place several in a heavy burlap bag. Then break the material with a rubber or wooden mallet on a sidewalk, patio, or other solid surface. Don't mix ceramics in the bag with glass–by the time the ceramics are the right size, your glass will be powder. When you're done, throw the bag or towel away or shake it out gently and store it for another project. Don't wash a towel and try to reuse it as a towel–it will still be filled with tiny, sharp shards.

The projects shown on these pages can enhance flowerpots, window boxes, outdoor furniture, mirror frames, or anything else you might want to try.

Tile Tabletop

Tile can rejuvenate an old table or at least add a little pizzazz to a piece of plain and inexpensive furniture.

If you're tiling a tabletop that's slightly warped, use small tile—it doesn't crack as easily as large tile. If the tabletop is severely warped, sand it with a belt sander and a coarse sanding belt to make it relatively flat. If the table will get a lot of use or will get wet, lay the tile with thinset mortar. For a table that's primarily decorative, use organic mastic as the adhesive.

Grouting the tile is messy work. You may want to take the table outside where the mess will be easier to clean up.

COVERING THE TABLE

1 Set out spaced tile in a dry layout, including any border tile, on the tabletop. When the layout looks right, mark the edges of at least every other tile and snap layout lines at the marks. Test the intersections with a framing square to make sure they're square.

2 Spread mortar on the table just up to your layout lines. If the space between layout lines is small, make a trowel by notching the edge of a plastic scraper. Starting in the center, set the field tiles. When the mortar is dry, set the border or edge tiles with the factory edge to the outside. Let the mortar cure, then grout the joints with a grout float. Clean the tiles and remove the haze with a soft rag.

TILE HOUSE NUMBERS

You'll find many styles of ceramic tiles with numbers in tile stores and home centers. The tiles make an attractive and durable address on your house, and the numbers are usually easier to read than the standard metal numerals. If you want something special, search on the Internet for handmade tiles.

All ceramic numerals go on with the same techniques. If you're setting the numbers in a frame, build the frame first, fasten it to the wall, then adhere the tiles with thinset or organic mastic, similar to the method shown for window rosettes on *page 79*. You can also mortar the tiles in the frame and fasten it to the wall with decorative screws through predrilled holes in the frame.

INSTALLING THE NUMBERS

❶ Lay out the numbers on a table or other flat surface, spacing them to allow for joints. Measure the layout and transfer the dimensions to the exterior wall surface. Keep the outline level.

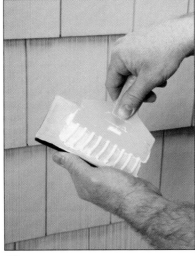

❷ On siding, use organic mastic to anchor the tiles. On a masonry wall, use thinset. On either type surface, back-butter the tiles and press them firmly onto the surface.

❸ Tape each tile in place as you set it. Let the adhesive cure for at least 12 hours, then remove the tape.

MOSAIC BIRDBATH

Browse through the garden section of your home center or a mail-order catalog, and you're sure to find a birdbath that would make a distinctive ornament for your yard. You might even find one all decked out in a mosaic design. But you can buy a plain one and a few tiles, then have all the fun of creating your own without paying the extra cost.

Wall tiles make excellent mosaics. They're soft, so they break easily, and they are just the right thickness. Keep your eye out for tile sales. Discount tiles are perfect for a decorative project. Pick three or four colors and throw in some glazed tiles for variation. Larger birdbaths will be easier to work with.

If your birdbath has a rim like the one shown above, square or rectangular tiles will look better around the rim than broken ceramics. Lay a string around the top edge to measure the circumference and divide its length by the width of the tile to determine how many you need. If

you still end up with a partial tile, adjust the grout lines a little to make everything come out right. You can also cut your own border tiles with a wet saw (but consider the rental costs to make sure it's worth it).

To find out how much tile you will need for the bottom of a round birdbath, square the radius (the distance from the center to the edge) and multiply that number by 3.14. Then divide that number by the area of one tile (multiply the tile length times width). Then double that amount and buy that many tiles. You'll need more than you might think because making mosaics wastes about half the tiles, and the bottom of the bowl is usually a section of a sphere, rather than a flat circle.

When you're breaking the tile in a burlap bag or a towel, put the bag or towel on a solid work surface; a patio or sidewalk is best. Break the tile with a rubber or wooden mallet until most of the pieces are 1 to 1½ inches wide.

LINING THE BIRDBATH

1 Lay the tiles around the rim first, back-buttering the pieces and pushing them into place. To get the tiles plumb and flush with the top edge of the rim, set a piece of scrap wood on the edge and push the tiles up to it. Back-butter the decorative center tile and install it in the bottom of the bowl.

2 Tumble your mosaic pieces in a paper bag to mix the colors randomly. Spread latex-modified thinset in the bowl with a notched plastic scraper or spatula. Then, working from the center to the rim, push the mosaics into the mortar. Make sure that their edges tilt only slightly, if at all. Try to space the pieces consistently so the grout will look even. Widely varying grout lines will make it look like you threw the pieces in without a plan. Let the mortar dry.

3 Mix grout and spread it on the mosaics with a spatula. Force the grout into the joints, then remove the excess with the spatula. Let the grout set about 15 minutes, then remove the remaining grout with a slightly dampened sponge. Let the grout set for another 5 to 10 minutes, then sponge it again. When the grout hardens, clean the surface with a plastic scrubber.

PRECAST BENCH

Precast concrete benches are right at home in a yard or garden. Put one at the end of a pathway to create a secluded retreat, or set one at the edge of a raised flower bed to take in the view while taking a quick break from planting or mulching. You can also arrange a few of them in a half circle to make an outdoor conversation area. These versatile benches are inexpensive, but most of them are pretty plain. Add style by dressing up a precast bench with ceramic tile.

Choose a bench that fits in with other features of your landscape. Bench styles differ mainly in the shape of the legs. You can tile the legs, too, on some benches with straight legs.

Once you decide on a bench, measure the seat slab and find tile that will fit the bench without any cutting if possible. Covering the surface with small or mosaic tiles should minimize the amount of cutting needed.

How you treat the edges will affect the amount of time you need to put into the project. You can leave cut or factory edges squared, but squared edges can easily chip. Bullnose tile, with its rounded edge, finishes your project nicely. If bullnose isn't available or is too expensive, you can round the edges of regular tiles with a masonry stone after the grout has set. Working in sections, use a long stroke and a rolling action to round the edges of the tile.

COVERING THE BENCH

1 Dry-lay the tile with spacers over the entire surface of the bench. If you'll have an odd number of rows, center the middle row. If you have an even number of rows, center the middle grout joint. Cut edge tiles if necessary. Then mark the edges of the tiles at each row and at each column. Remove the tiles and set them aside.

2 Snap parallel chalk lines between the marks, squaring them with a framing square. Use these layout lines as guides when you set the tile.

3 Working between your layout lines, comb latex-modified mortar onto the bench with a notched plastic trowel. Lay the tiles with a slight twist and embed them with a beater block. Insert spacers to keep the tiles evenly spaced and line up the edges with a metal straightedge. Lay the edge tiles with their cut edge facing inward.

4 Lift every third or fourth tile to make sure the back is fully covered. Back-butter the tiles when necessary and reset them. Clean excess mortar from the joints with a spacer, and scrape excess from the outside edges. Let the mortar cure overnight.

5 Grout the surface with a latex-modified grout (sanded or unsanded). When the grout is hard enough so you can dent it slightly with a thumbnail, wipe it with a dampened sponge and remove the haze. Scrub off stubborn spots with a plastic scrubber.

ACCENT PAVERS FOR YOUR GARDEN PATH

These colorful precast stepping-stones can turn a drab series of concrete steps into an enchanting walkway. You can use tiles of different thicknesses for this mosaic project. Tile edges that rise above the surface will help increase traction on the paver.

Make stepping-stone pieces larger than those for a birdbath or mosaic table. Before you start, set the stepping-stone on a piece of cardboard and trace its outline. Dry-lay the mosaics on this template until you get a pattern you like. Then transfer the mosaics to the mortared paver one by one.

TILING THE PAVER

1 Soak each precast stepping-stone in water for a minute or two so it won't draw the moisture out of the mortar. Set one stone in a plastic tub while you're tiling another. Mix up the amount of latex-modified thinset you can use before it sets up and spread a ¼ to ½ inch coat on one stone with a notched plastic trowel.

2 Take up each mosaic from the cardboard template and press it into the mortar, leaving a ⅛- to ¼-inch gap for grout. If a piece is too low, lift it and back-butter it with mortar. Scrape away excess mortar with a spatula. Let the mortar cure overnight.

3 Mix latex-modified grout and force it into the joints with the spatula or a grout float. Remove the excess with the edge of the spatula or a float, and smooth grout on the edges of the pattern.

4 Let the grout set for 10 to 15 minutes (or as recommended by the manufacturer), then clean off the stones with a wet sponge. Rinse the sponge often, but don't pull the grout from the gaps. Let the stones dry 24 to 48 hours, then buff with a soft cloth.

MOSAIC TABLETOP

Undecorated square tiles make an attractive tabletop, but their rigid shape somewhat limits their design potential. Colorful mosaics, by contrast, open up endless possibilities. Attach cement backerboard to a thin sheet of exterior plywood on top of your table. Sketch a theme—floral, geometric, waves, or minimalist lines—with colored chalk. You can draw broad outlines at this point, without detail. You will probably alter the design somewhat as you lay the tiles, anyway. Choose a color scheme.

Break the material into pieces ½ to 1 inch wide at their largest dimension. Make precise shapes or fit the pieces next to each other with tile nippers. Most table mosaics look best with relatively small pieces and tight grout lines. Lay out the pieces in a dry run on the backerboard, then set the design into the mortar. Tweezers make the job easier.

TILING THE TABLETOP

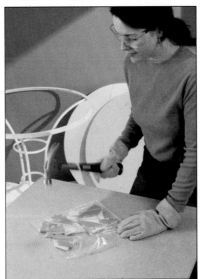

1 Gather up all the raw material for your mosaics. Different kinds of material break into different sizes, so break up each kind separately in a bag or wrapped in a towel. Break the material into ½- to 1-inch pieces.

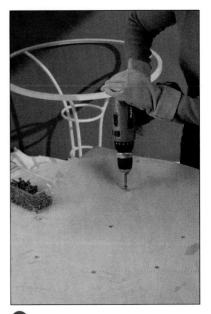

2 Cut a sheet of thin water-resistant exterior-grade plywood the same size as the tabletop. Attach a piece of cement backerboard to the plywood. Sketch your design on the backerboard with colored chalk. Don't be afraid to wipe the chalk away and change the pattern as you go.

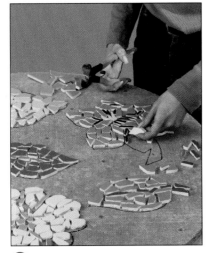

3 Dry-fit your mosaics on your sketch, using tile nippers to cut the pieces when necessary. Be sure to allow about ¼ inch between them.

4 With a notched trowel, mix and apply thinset to a small section of the backerboard. Set the tiles into the thinset mortar. Use a beater block to level the tiles.

5 Press grout into the joints with a grout float, and following the manufacturer's instructions, let the grout set, then clean it with a sponge. Be sure to scrub the haze off with a soft rag. Finally, seal the surface.

MAKING MOSAIC MAGIC

Mosaics of broken ceramic, china, or glass can transform almost any object into a decorative accent you can use indoors or out.

Your container garden will take on added

▲ A mosaic rim turns an ordinary flowerpot into a decorative planter suitable for deck or patio.

appeal with a few clay pots adorned in a colorful design. Make your own low-cost wall mural from broken-tile mosaics rather than buying a commercial one. Set a mosaic pattern in a floor with broken floor tiles.

For either outdoor or indoor projects that will get wet, use latex-modified thinset. For projects that won't get wet, you can use organic mastic or mosaic glue. Mastic and glue, however, are applied thinner than mortar and don't allow you much leeway to adjust for any

▶ A concrete turtle is a charming garden ornament, but it becomes an eye-catching conversation piece with a mosaic shell.

pieces that are thinner or thicker than the others. Mortar will also adhere to all the curvature of pieces broken from pots or plates. Mastic and glue may grab only the edges.

It's usually best to use both a white mortar and a white grout—or mortar and grout of the same color. Colored mortar that's left in the joints can mottle the grout. You won't have to worry about getting all the excess mortar out of all the joints between the tiles if you use mortar and grout of the same color.

Breaking mosaics and mixing powdered mortars and grouts raise dust, so wear a dust mask while you work. Wear gloves when mixing cement-based products—they are caustic.

Most mosaic projects call for thinner ridges in the mortar than other tile installations. Ridges of about $\frac{3}{16}$ inch will be just right. If you can't find the square applicator made for such hobby projects, you can buy several inexpensive plastic scrapers at your hardware store and notch the edges to make homemade trowels. (Get more than one scraper—even if you're only planning one project now, you're bound to think of others, and the scrapers will wear out.)

Breaking your material into pieces of the right size is only the first step. Most of these random shapes will not be usable right out of the bag. Buy high-quality tile nippers with tough steel jaws—the cost will be well worth it because your hands will not tire as easily. Put a glove on the hand squeezing the nippers for a little extra padding, and wear eye protection when nipping the tile; small pieces can fly out faster than you can blink. Don't insert a tile shard completely in the jaws of the nippers; you will quickly tire out your hands and end up with mostly fractured tiles. Use just a little pressure to snap the tile about $\frac{1}{16}$ inch where you want it. For larger pieces, work the nippers across the cut a little at a time.

Setting in small pieces can be tedious work, but you can make it easier with large tweezers or spring-loaded needle-nose pliers. Be sure to let the mortar or mastic cure completely before grouting. Mist the edges of the tile lightly with water before you grout so they won't draw as much water from the grout.

▲ A mosaic birdhouse with a conical roof takes a lot of planning and cutting, but the result—a colorful accent to use outside or on an indoor windowsill—is well worth the effort.

◀ Tiling a mirror in an elaborate pattern will take some time, but you'll be rewarded with a stunning accessory for any room. Tape heavy butcher's paper to the mirror before tiling the frame—or remove the mirror—so you won't scratch it with mortar or grout.

CHAPTER HIGHLIGHTS

With this chapter, you'll see how to
install ceramic tile in a variety of
outdoor settings, starting with
pouring a new concrete slab, then
with techniques for tiling a patio,
steps, and an outdoor kitchen.

TILING OUTDOOR PROJECTS

All outdoor tile installations require a base made of concrete. Some also need footings, extra thick sections reinforced with rebar that go deeper into the ground. Although all concrete looks the same, modifications to the mix can match it to weather conditions or project size.

Air bubbles in the mix (called air entrainment) help keep concrete from freezing. Accelerators help it set up faster in cold weather, and retardants slow curing in hot weather. Water reducers make the mix more workable, reducing time and labor on large projects. Ask for advice when you order concrete from your ready-mix supplier.

If you're mixing your own concrete in a wheelbarrow, protect your yard from ruts with 2×12 ramps and runways. If the forms for your slab will be temporary, coat them with new or used motor oil or a commercial releasing agent so you can pull them away easily after the concrete has cured. If your forms will stay in place as a frame around the slab, use redwood, cedar, or pressure-treated lumber rated for ground contact. Duct-tape the top edges to keep them from staining when you pour. And don't pour new concrete against concrete that has already set up; the resulting joint can easily fracture.

TILING A PATIO

If you have an existing slab that's the right size for a patio and is in good shape, you can tile right over it. You can also tile over existing brick and tile. Make sure the surface is level and flat (with no high spots more than ⅛ inch in 10 feet). Repair cracks in the surface.

Inspect cracks closely. If the slab edges are pulled apart on the same plane, chances are it's not an indication of a structural problem. But one edge that's lower than another could indicate a structural problem. And if whole sections sag, you'll have to tear out the old slab and pour a new one. A slab that's crowned in the center for drainage is suitable for tiling if the crowning is gradual.

You can repair minor holes or flaking with the techniques shown here. If the edges are chipped, knock away any loose material with a small sledge and brickset, then repair the edge as if it were the edge of a concrete step (see *pages 124–125)*.

Most codes require control joints for slabs larger than 8 feet. No matter what you do, concrete will eventually crack. Control joints allow the slab to move without cracking the tile.

If you're pouring a new slab, put control joints in the surface with a jointing trowel. If your old slab doesn't have control joints, rent a masonry saw and cut your own—about ¾ inch deep on a 4-inch slab. Some codes consider the installation of a slab to be a major home improvement that requires a permit. Consult your building department before you start.

REPAIRING AN OLD SLAB

1 Inspect the surface of the slab by working a carpenter's level across it in 6-foot squares. Mark cracks, high spots, and other defects with a carpenter's pencil.

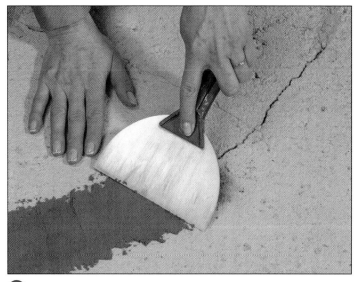

2 Repair the cracks first. Using a small sledge and a cold chisel, shape the crack so the bottom is wider than the top. This provides a key to hold the mortar securely. Blow the dust out and mist the crack with water. Push quick-setting hydraulic cement or thinset into the crack with a trowel and feather the edges until the patch is level with the surrounding surface. When the mortar has cured, apply a roll-on isolation membrane (see *page 125*).

3 Fill depressions with self-leveling compound or trowel on a skim coat of thinset. If you use thinset, feather the edges even with the floor. Self-leveling compound will do this on its own.

4 Wear down high spots with a right-angle grinder fitted with a masonry-grit abrasive wheel. Vacuum and damp-mop the slab thoroughly.

REMOVING AN OLD SLAB

Removing a slab is hard work; you may want to hire someone to do the job. You'll need a jackhammer (you can rent one) or a 10-pound sledgehammer and crowbars. If the slab is thicker than 4 inches, hire a contractor.

Start at a corner and crack sections until they're small enough that you can put them in a wheelbarrow. Pry out each section using a crowbar as a lever, so it does most of the work. You'll find that prying up concrete is easier than cracking it.

POURING A NEW SLAB

You can avoid hours of tiling time if you design your slab so its dimensions are the same as an even multiple of tiles and spacers. That way, you won't have to cut tiles for the edges. Once the slab cures, you can even out slight size discrepancies (concrete is not a precise medium) by adjusting the width of the grout joints a little.

You can also save time by using the right tools when you excavate the site. Removing sod is part art, part science–and a lot of work. Renting a sod cutter will make the job easier.

To remove sod without a cutter, use a square-nose shovel or spade to edge the site and cut the sod into strips. It works better than a roundnose shovel. A spade will cut the roots from the soil faster than either type of shovel. When you take up the sod, keep the angle of the spade low. Cut the roots, then remove the sod in clumps, if you don't want to reuse it, or strips, if you do. If you'll reuse it, but not right away, roll the sod and store it in a shaded spot.

Once you remove the sod, till the soil. Set the tiller to the depth of the excavation (the thickness of the slab plus the gravel base), and make several passes over the area. This will loosen the soil and make it much easier to remove. Plan ahead so you know what you'll do with the soil you dig out. That will save you from having to move it twice.

Patios must slope about 1 inch every 4 feet so the water will run off. Build this slope into your excavation. You can set up grid lines about every 4 feet across the site and measure down at various points to get the proper slope, or you can use a slope gauge. Tape a 2-foot level to a longer 2×4 with a ½-inch drill bit under one end of the level, then set this assembly in the excavation as you dig. The drill bit raises the end of the level so that when the bubble is centered, the slope is correct.

Batterboards ensure that the corners are square. You need them for a large site, but if you're only adding a small pad–to build a grill next to an existing patio, for instance–lay out the corners using a 4×8 plywood sheet. After you've laid out the site, take the batterboards apart and cut them into braces for your forms.

TYPICAL OUTDOOR SLAB CONSTRUCTION

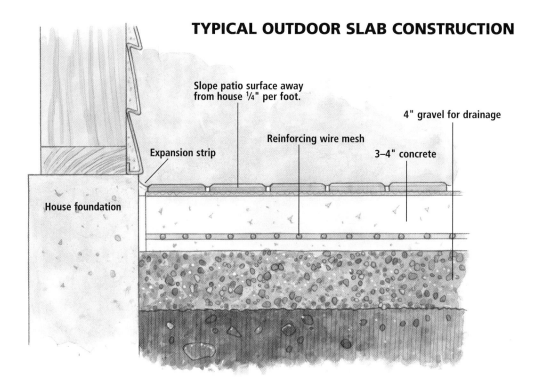

Slope patio surface away from house ¼" per foot.

4" gravel for drainage

Reinforcing wire mesh

Expansion strip

3–4" concrete

House foundation

LAYING OUT THE SITE

① Assemble batterboards from 2×4s and drive them into the ground 3 to 4 feet beyond the corners of your proposed slab. Tie mason's lines tightly between the batterboards and square the lines with a 3-4-5 triangle *(below)*. At each corner, suspend a plumb bob just touching the intersection of the lines. Stake the spot where the plumb bob rests to represent the outside corners of the excavation.

② Run mason's lines between the ground stakes and pull them tight. Then mark the ground along the line with upside-down spray paint. Untie the mason's lines from the batterboards to get them out of the way. Cut the sod along the ground and then into 12-inch strips with a square shovel. If you will reuse the sod, dislodge the roots with a spade and roll up the strips.

LAYING OUT A PATIO SITE

If patio is detached from house, use batterboards here.

6. Tie lines between stakes and mark on the ground with paint.

5. Drop plumb bob to mark corners with stakes.

3'

4'

5'

4. Square corners with 3-4-5 triangle method, adjusting lines as necessary.

3. Level lines by adjusting height on crossbars.

Batterboards

Line level

2. Tie mason's lines to nails centered on crosspieces.

1. Set preliminary corner stakes and drive batterboards 3 to 4 feet beyond stakes.

POURING A NEW SLAB (CONTINUED)

PREPARING THE BASE

1 Stake 2× forms with the inside edge just under the ground line. Attach stakes with deck screws at the corners and every 2 to 4 feet between them. Strengthen splices by nailing on ½-inch plywood cleats.

2 Spread a 4-inch gravel base (check codes first), then pack it with a power tamper. Lay 6×6-inch 10/10 reinforcing wire on 2-inch dobies (supports for rebar or reinforcing wire), tying every fourth or fifth intersection of the mesh to the dobies.

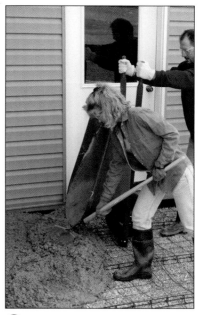

3 Start pouring concrete in the corner farthest from the truck or mixer. Pour concrete to the top of the forms, then push it into the edges with a shovel or garden rake. Work a shovel or 2×4 up and down to consolidate the concrete. Add the next load of concrete as soon as you've spread the first one and have begun to screed it. Pour each load where the previous one ends.

4 Screed the concrete level with a long 2×4, working the screed on top of the forms with a side-to-side motion. Fill in low spots and screed them again.

5 Smooth the concrete with floats. Where you can reach from the edges of the slab, use a hand float. Use a bull float where you can't reach from the edge. Hold the float flat as you move it across the surface in wide arcs. Then tilt it slightly and work the surface again.

6 Mortar will stick better to a surface that's slightly rough. Brooming creates just the right tooth. Drag a dampened garage broom across the concrete while it's still wet.

7 To cure the concrete and minimize cracking, cover the slab with plastic or straw. The covering slows the evaporation of moisture from the surface. Weight the edges of plastic with stones or boards. From time to time over the next week, sprinkle the surface with water. Don't use a curing agent—thinset will not stick to treated concrete. Snap layout lines when the slab has cured.

MIXING YOUR OWN CONCRETE

On sites less than 100 square feet, it's economical to mix concrete in a rented power mixer. Combine one part portland cement, two parts sand, three parts gravel in the mixer, and add one-fourth part water a little at a time.

SETTING THE TILE

Snap chalk lines at the midpoints of the length and width of the slab. Square these lines with a 3-4-5 triangle, adjusting them as necessary (see *page 115*). If you won't need cut tiles, you can get started right away–snap additional layout lines, spread the mortar, and lay the tile.

If your slab requires cut edge tiles, dry-lay tiles and spacers (no mortar) on each line, pushing them back and forth until you have even tiles at both ends. Then snap additional parallel lines at distances equal to the dimensions of your tile, including the grout joint.

It's best to apply mortar when temperatures are between 60 and 70 degrees. Don't work in direct sunlight–the mortar will set up too quickly.

Start with enough mortar to lay just a few tiles. As you work, you'll develop a rhythm. Work in sections you can complete in about 10 minutes. When you press the tiles into place, mortar will squeeze up between them. If the mortar comes up more than half the thickness of the tile, you're using too much pressure. Scrape it out by dragging a spacer through the joint. Keep the tiles in line with spacers–insert them on end so they will be easier to take out. Remove them from the tile when the mortar begins to set–pulling them out after the mortar cures will be difficult and time consuming.

As you approach an edge, have the cut tiles ready so you can set them in place without searching for them or having to cut new ones.

Concrete is hard–wear knee pads for comfort and protection.

INSTALLING THE TILE

1 Spread and comb thinset at the intersection of your center-most layout lines, but don't cover the lines. Then set each tile on the lines with a slight twist. Embed the tile with a rubber mallet and beater block, leveling it with the rest of the tiles.

2 In the first section, lift every tenth tile or so and make sure mortar covers its entire surface. If it doesn't, back-butter additional mortar and reset the tile. After the first section, you'll get to know how thick to trowel on the adhesive without lifting the tile. If a tile is too low, pull it up, apply more mortar, and reset it. If a tile is too high, scrape off excess mortar and reset it.

3 Continue spreading mortar and laying the tile in sections, but do not mortar the control joints. When you've finished a section and the mortar has begun to set, pull the spacers and clean the joints by running a spacer between them. Let the mortar cure.

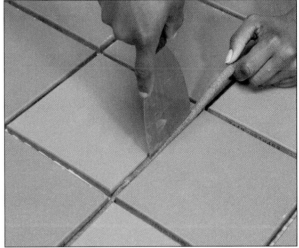

4 Stuff foam backer rod into the control joints with a wide putty knife or margin trowel. Caulk the gap in the tiles above the joint with a high-quality silicone exterior caulk that's the same color as your grout.

CUTTING PATIO TILE

1 Set the tile you want to cut on top of the last set tile, with the edges lined up exactly. Place another tile on top of that one and against the wall, then mark the cut line with a pencil.

2 Use a wet saw to cut patio tiles. Set the tile against the fence so the cut line is in line with the blade, start the saw, then push the tile into the blade.

GROUTING THE TILE

1 Mix only the amount of grout you can work with before it sets. Spread grout across the tiles, forcing it into the joints with the trailing edge of the grout float. Work diagonally across the surface to fill the joints. Clean each section before grouting the next one.

2 When all the joints in a section are full, rinse the grout float in a bucket of warm, clean water and scrape excess grout from the section, keeping the float almost perpendicular to the surface. Don't press the float into the joints—it will remove the grout from the joints.

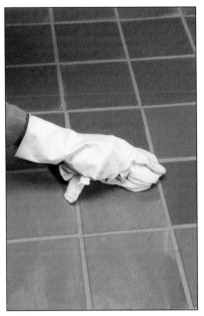

③ Test the grout to make sure it's set up, then wipe the surface with a damp (not wet) sponge. The more you change the water, the less haze you'll have to remove in the next step.

④ Scrub the haze off the tiles with a clean soft cloth. Scrub hard if necessary— you won't damage the tiles or the grout.

⑤ After the mortar has set, caulk the joints where the patio meets the foundation of the house and smooth the bead with a wet finger.

GROUTING WIDE JOINTS

Some styles of tile look better with wide grout joints. Saltillo tiles and other handmade materials, for example, look best with grout joints at least ⅜ inch wide. A grout float will pull the grout out of joints this wide as you apply it, so you'll have to use a grout bag for

these types of tile. Load the bag with grout and squeeze the bag as you draw its nozzle along the length of the joint. Stop just short of filling the joint completely, then tool the joints smooth with the rounded end of a trowel handle.

TILING A FLAGSTONE PATIO

Like ceramic tile, mortared flagstone needs a solid, level concrete slab. Prepare an existing slab or pour a new one as needed.

Take time to lay out a pleasing pattern. Once it's mortared, it will be difficult to change. Try to visualize the slab in sections, not as individual stones. Vary the size, shape, and color as you go, keeping the spacing a uniform ½ to ¾ inch. (But set cut stone tighter or with no gap.) From time to time, stand back to check your work. Rearrange it if you don't like it.

Use Type M mortar; it has high compressive strength that will keep the stones from cracking. Clean off any spills with a wet broom in one section before you start the next. Don't wait until you've laid the entire patio because the mortar will set on the first stones and won't come off.

The thickest stone determines the height of the entire patio, so set it first and use a height gauge to level the adjoining stones. Keep the rest of the surface on the same plane, using a carpenter's level.

INSTALLING THE TILE

1 Set out the stones on the slab in a trial run. Put larger stones along the edge, smaller ones in between. Rearrange them until you get a pattern you like. Cut stones to fit, as necessary. Then lift the stones off in 3×3-foot sections and lay them on the grass next to the site in the same pattern.

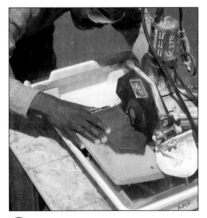

2 Mix up enough mortar for the open section, dump it on the slab, and spread it to a consistent 1-inch thickness. Then comb it out in ridges.

3 When you pick out the stones from your pattern on the grass, set the large stones first, using a height gauge to keep them at the same height. Push the stones down; don't slide them. When the large stones are set, fill the spaces between them with smaller stones, embedding them with a rubber mallet. Let the mortar cure.

CUTTING FLAGSTONE

4 Fill the joints with a mortar bag. Minimize staining by not overfilling the joints, and clean spilled mortar off the tile right away with a wet sponge. When the mortar holds a thumbprint with slight pressure, finish the joints with a jointing tool. Cover the surface with plastic or burlap (mist it periodically to keep it wet) and let it cure for three to four days.

1 Mark the contour of the cut on the stone with a china marker. You can estimate where the line should fall or set the adjoining stone on top. Tap a brickset along the line to score it.

2 Cut the stone with a wet saw. Or, you can set the stone with the mark along a pipe or the edge of another stone, and break the stone with a single strong blow. Then shape the edge with a mason's hammer until it fits into your pattern.

TILING OUTDOOR STEPS

Durable and weather-resistant, concrete is ideal for outdoor stairs. But it's also drab and unattractive. Dress up those stairs with stylish ceramic tile.

Prepare the steps as you would a concrete slab: Level depressions, patch cracks, and grind down high spots. Pay special attention to the edges of steps. The opposite page shows how to repair them so there won't be weak spots that could cause the tile to crack. Use sand-mix mortar for these repairs; patching compound will not stand up to constant use. Wash oily spots with a solution of trisodium phosphate (TSP) or use a concrete cleaner your home center employee recommends.

Keep the steps safe by using nonslip tiles made for stairs, and radius caps over the tread nosing. If you can't get the style of radius caps that you want, some V-cap styles will make a good substitute. If neither is available, use standard field tile and round the edges. For extra safety, install slip-resistant inserts in the tread edges. These metal channels slip under the tread and hold a replaceable plastic or rubber insert that covers the nosing.

You can also use self-stick abrasive strips that are made for this purpose. These strips wear off in time, and require replacement. Glazed tiles are dangerously slick when wet so they should be used only on the risers.

INSTALLING THE TILE

1 The edges of concrete steps will show some degree of damage sooner or later. Begin your repair by chipping away loose concrete with a brickset and small sledgehammer.

2 Sweep or blow away the dust and loose material, then set a 2×8 against the front of the damaged edge and support it with bricks or blocks. Wet the area with fine spray from a garden hose, then fill the recess with concrete and smooth it along the top of the form.

3 When the repaired edges have cured, patch any cracks and roll on an isolation membrane over them.

4 Dry-lay the tiles on the steps to make sure everything fits correctly. Then, starting on the bottom riser, spread and comb Type M mortar with the notched edge of the trowel. Set spacers between the tiles and along the bottom edges. Then set the radius cap on the front edge of the first step. Tile up the steps in the same fashion. When the mortar has cured, grout the tiles with a grout bag, as shown on *page 121*.

TILING AN OUTDOOR KITCHEN

A basic outdoor kitchen only needs space for a grill. But your kitchen can include a prep sink, refrigerator, rotisserie, and storage areas. No matter how complex your kitchen, the basic steps in tiling it are the same.

To build an outdoor kitchen, lay out and pour a slab and footings as local codes require. Build block walls, making sure the bay for the grill meets the manufacturer's specifications. Then build the countertop base from plywood, backerboard, and metal lath. Or, you can use 3-inch, 3×3-foot square precast concrete stepping-stones available at most home centers. They make an excellent tile base, and the 3-inch thickness works well with 8½-inch concrete block to bring your countertop height to a comfortable 36 inches.

OUTDOOR KITCHEN BASE

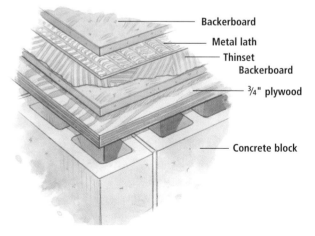

Backerboard
Metal lath
Thinset
Backerboard
¾" plywood
Concrete block

INSTALLING THE TILE

1 Build a base from concrete block, then cut ¾-inch exterior-grade plywood, metal lath, and backerboard to fit each section of the countertop. Anchor the plywood to the block webs with concrete screws (not lag shields), mortar the plywood, then install the backerboard and metal lath.

2 Using the same techniques as for a wall (*pages 70–71*) and a countertop (*pages 72–73*), dry-lay the tile to check the layout. Then snap layout lines. Trowel thinset or the adhesive recommended by the manufacturer on the concrete block and lay the tile from the bottom up.

3 Spread and comb a level coat of latex-modified thinset on the backerboard on top and set the field tile. Finish the front edge of the countertop with bullnose tile, back-buttering each tile and pressing it into place. Use masking tape or screws (as shown) to hold the tiles until the mortar sets.

4 When the mortar cures, grout the top tile with a latex-modified grout. Let the grout cure, clean it, then drop in the grill. Grout the sides and front with a mortar bag. Let the mortar set up slightly, then tool it with a jointing tool.

CHAPTER HIGHLIGHTS

Regular cleaning helps keep any tiled surface in good condition. If the tile surface becomes damaged, you may need to remove and replace one or more tiles. This chapter shows you how to maintain and repair any tile.

CARING FOR YOUR TILE SURFACE

Tile floor and wallcoverings are relatively low-maintenance surfaces. In most rooms, regularly vacuuming and damp-mopping floors and wiping walls with a damp sponge will keep them from deteriorating.

In showers and baths, however, soap film, mineral deposits, and mildew can cause problems. For these, you'll need a cleaning agent. Many commercial products are available, or you can use a mixture of vinegar and water or bleach and water. Toothbrushes are great for cleaning grout lines.

Damage on the surface may indicate more serious problems underneath. Always try to find the cause of the damage before making repairs.

If water is the problem, check for damaged caulk or sealant, or uncaulked joints at fixtures. A spongy surface can indicate rot; remove a few tiles to check. If you find rot you'll have to remove the entire surface, repair or replace the substrate, and put in new tile.

If you need to remove a stain, ask your tile supplier for a commercial stain-removal agent made for your tile.

Replacing Grout

Because grout takes up only small spaces between tiles and it stains easily, you might think it's a relatively soft material. If you've never had to clean out stained or damaged grout joints, you may be surprised at how tough grout is.

A rotary hand tool makes removal go much more quickly than chipping away by hand. One of these high-speed tools—equipped with a diamond grinding burr—can cut through a lot of grout in a small amount of time. If you don't own one and have to remove a lot of grout, the time it will save you will be well worth its moderate price.

Use a burr small enough to fit into the joints without marring the tile edges. Grind out a small area and change burrs if your first choice is too large. Keep the tool moving—its high speed generates heat, which won't affect the tile, but will quickly wear out the burr. You don't have to remove the grout down to the wall underneath—stop when you reach clean, solid material and have a groove deep enough to give tooth for the new grout. Wear a dust mask and eye protection—safety goggles with side protectors—to keep flying chips and grout dust out of your eyes.

Try to determine what caused the grout to deteriorate. A few small areas may not indicate a problem, but large cracks not only may have been caused by a structural problem, they may have let water behind the tile. If so, you should remove the tile and the wall surface down to the studs and start over.

If the grout is stained or mildewed, clean it with a commercial product made specifically for grout. Most of these solutions, available at your home center, contain bleaches and other chemicals, so wear eye protection, gloves, and old clothes (long-sleeve shirts) when using them. Make sure you have plenty of ventilation in the room. Replace stained grout only if cleaners can't remove the stains.

If you're replacing only a small number of joints, try to match the color of the existing grout. Dig out a chip of grout and take it to your retailer and have someone there match the color. (Don't take the grout dust—it's not a reliable indicator of the color.) You may be able to mix two grouts together to get a good match.

REGROUTING

1 If you have just a small amount of grout to repair, you can remove it with a grout saw (see *opposite page*). For larger jobs or wide joints, grind out the grout with a rotary hand tool fitted with a diamond burr. Choose a bit slightly smaller than an empty grout joint and work the tool with two hands. Chip out mortared joints with a cold chisel.

2 Brush the joints clean with a stiff scrub brush and flood the surface with a wet sponge to wash away loose grout. Let the joints dry overnight, then mix up enough grout to repair the area and apply it with a grout float.

3 After completing one section, scrape off the excess grout with the float, holding it almost perpendicular. Let the grout set up, then dampen a sponge and clean off the residue. Then, grout and clean the remaining sections.

4 Wait for the grout to set up before cleaning so the grout won't be pulled from the joints. When the grout is hard enough that you can't make an impression in it with your thumbnail, you can start cleaning.

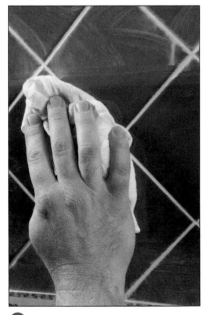

5 After you have cleaned the entire wall, scrub the haze from the surface with a soft cloth. Seal the grout (and the tile, if necessary) with the product recommended by the manufacturer.

USING A GROUT SAW

If you have only a small area that needs repair, you can remove the grout with a grout saw—a small, handheld tool available at hardware stores. Hold the tool with the blade flat against the joint and perpendicular to the surface. Work the tool back and forth in the joint until you have removed about half the grout.

REPAIRING DAMAGED CERAMIC TILE

Tile may be tough, but it's not indestructible. Falling objects can chip it or crack it. Poor adhesive bonds often cause the tile to loosen, and voids or imperfections in the substrate under the tile–which leave it unsupported–can lead to either cracks or loose tiles. Defects in the tile surface could indicate structural problems that need attention. If damage is widespread or frequent, you need to find the cause.

An improper grout mix or the absence of expansion joints can cause joints to crack. If the grout is soft and powdery in one area, check the rest of the surface; then remove the defective grout and replace it. If the cracked grout is firm, remove it and fill the joint with a matching colored grout.

A faulty adhesive bond or an underlying crack can cause tiles to crack on a long length of floor. Before you remove the tiles, tap them lightly with a metal object, such as a wrench. If you hear a hollow sound, the bond is probably at fault, and a thorough cleaning and new mortar will fix the problem. If the floor sounds solid, the bond is probably solid, but you may have an underlying crack in the substrate. To properly repair a cracked slab, you'll have to remove tiles even if they aren't damaged so you can get at the crack along its entire length and isolate it with a membrane.

Repairing the problem, of course, begins with removing the tile and grout. After you have taken up the tile, you can chip out the grout with a narrow cold chisel, but you may need a grout saw or rotary hand tool to get it all. Force the new grout into the joint with your finger and shape it to match the rest with a wet sponge. Replace damaged stone tile using the same techniques.

REPLACING A WALL TILE

① To make sure you remove the damaged tile without cracking the others, isolate it by scoring the grout with a carbide grout saw (or rotary hand tool). Protect the floor, tub, sink, or countertop with heavy paper.

② Break the damaged tile with a hammer and cold chisel, and remove the pieces, working from the center of the tile to the edges.

  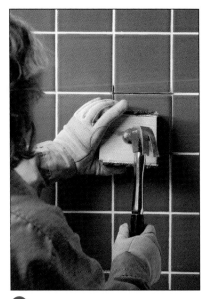

3 Pry out the broken pieces with a putty knife or margin trowel, then scrape the old adhesive from the wall.

4 Back-butter the new tile with the same adhesive or mortar used on the old tile. If you don't know what mortar was originally used, use thinset.

5 Press the new tile in place and set it with a beater block; use a straightedge to make sure it's level with the rest of the tiles. Center the new tile in the recess by driving brads part way into the joints. Tape the tile until the mortar cures, then regrout the tile.

REPLACING A FLOOR TILE

1 Grind out the grout from the joint along the entire length of the crack, plus at least one tile beyond those damaged. Apply a liquid isolation membrane.

2 Trowel thinset on the isolation membrane and back-butter each tile. Set the tiles and level them. Grout and clean when the mortar is dry.

MAINTAINING RESILIENT TILE

Resilient tiles now available have prefinished coatings made to take almost any amount of wear and tear.

With most resilient tiles, all you have to do is keep them clean. Grit and dust will do more damage to resilients than anything else. They wear away the shine gradually so you don't notice it until it's too late. Vacuuming with a canister vacuum and a brush (not a beater bar) and periodic damp-mopping will keep a resilient floor in tip-top shape. Establish a regular cleaning schedule for the floor, and clean up spills or dirty tracks immediately.

If you need a cleaning solution for an unusually soiled area, use one recommended or made by the tile manufacturer. Products formulated for all floors may contain chemicals that could dull the surface of your tile.

The chemicals in vinyl tile may interact with other synthetic products, especially the rubber backings on area rugs. Many rubber backings stain vinyl. Check with the tile manufacturer or retailer before laying a rubber-backed rug on resilient tile.

Self-stick felt and fiber pads made to keep furniture legs from scratching a floor can themselves do harm. When dust and grit get in them, they abrade the floor like fine sandpaper. Replace the pads with vinyl floor protectors that won't collect dirt and grit. You can remove some minor scuffing with a tile cleaner and #0000 steel wool. Rub gently.

And you really shouldn't wax no-wax floors. No-wax flooring is finished with either a polyurethane or vinyl coating that only needs damp-mopping. If you apply wax to either of the finishes, the resulting surface will be duller than the original and more slippery. Wax also attracts and holds dust and dirt more readily than the factory finish.

REMOVING STAINS FROM VINYL TILE

STAIN	REMOVE WITH
Asphalt, shoe polish	Citrus-based cleaner or mineral spirits
Candle wax	Scrape carefully with plastic spatula
Crayon	Mineral spirits or manufacturer's cleaner
Grape juice, wine, mustard	Full-strength bleach or manufacturer's recommended cleaner
Heel marks	Nonabrasive household cleaner; if stain remains, use rubbing alcohol
Lipstick	Rubbing alcohol or mineral spirits
Nail polish	Nail polish remover
Paint or varnish	Wipe with water or mineral spirits while still wet; if dry, scrape with a thin plastic spatula; if stain still shows, rub with rubbing alcohol
Pen ink	Citrus-based cleaner, rubbing alcohol, or mineral spirits
Permanent marker	Mineral spirits, nail polish remover, or rubbing alcohol
Rust	Oxalic acid and water (1 part acid to 10 parts water); extremely caustic–follow all directions

After removing the stain, wipe off cleaner residue with a damp cloth.

REPLACING VINYL TILE

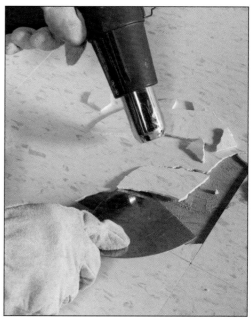

❶ To remove a damaged vinyl tile, soften the adhesive with a hair dryer or heat gun and pry up the tile a piece at a time. Vinyl tile won't come up in one piece—it will tear and leave small chunks stuck in the adhesive. Scrape the adhesive from the floor.

2 Spread adhesive into the recess with a notched trowel or notch the end of a plastic scraper and use it to comb the adhesive.

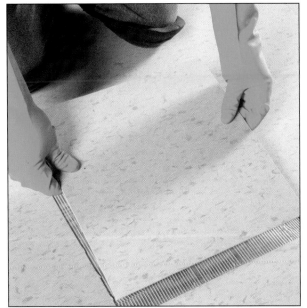

3 Check to make sure the orientation of the tile corresponds to the pattern of the floor, then set the tile at a slight angle with one edge tight against the other and lower the tile into place.

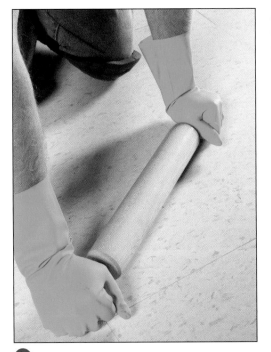

4 Warm the new tile slightly with a hair dryer, then roll it with a rolling pin to embed it into the adhesive.

PREVENTING DAMAGE TO VINYL TILE

Damp-mop and vacuum your vinyl floor regularly, and you can put off repair or replacement for many years to come. Vinyl floors, however, are prone to dents and scuffs. When you're moving the appliances back onto your new floor, use an appliance dolly or lay plywood sheets on the floor and walk the unit across the sheets. If you have furniture with single casters, replace them with double casters. Keep furniture legs from making an impression on your floor with vinyl floor protectors. Dust off the bottom of the protectors to keep them from scratching the floor when you move the furniture.

MAINTAINING LAMINATE TILE

A tough melamine wear coat protects laminate tile from heavy usage, and it withstands denting more than any other material except ceramic and stone tile. You won't be able to get the rare dent out, but you can repair scratches.

Protect the floor so it won't get scratched in the first place. Use area rugs at entrances to trap dirt before it gets onto the floor. Sweep or vacuum the floor daily to remove grit, and if something spills, wipe it up immediately. Clean the residue with a spray cleaner recommended by the laminate manufacturer.

Once a week, damp-mop the floor with a mild cleaning solution. Vacuum the floor before damp-mopping, or you'll just move a dirty haze around with the mop.

If you're moving furniture, use an appliance dolly; or if you're doing the job by hand, ask someone to help. Lift the furniture, don't slide it. Protect the floor with vinyl furniture coasters under the legs. If you have plastic furniture rollers, replace them with rubber rollers.

Humidity affects laminate flooring more than other materials, especially at the joints. Humidity of 50 percent keeps the joints closed, which prevents dirt from accumulating between the tiles. After coming in from the rain or snow, mop up excess water—it can seep into the joints and warp the floor. And, most important, don't wax laminate tile. Wax can make some laminates dangerously slippery. Wax will dull the factory-bright wear coat of any laminate.

To remove a damaged tile in a snap-together installation, unsnap the damaged tiles outward from the wall, install the new tile, then reassemble the floor. In a glued floor, you must cut the damaged tile out at the joint and glue in a replacement tile. Making the replacement look like the original can be difficult, so you may want to hire a repair specialist.

If you do the work yourself, set your saw just to the depth of the tile (about $5/16$ inch) and put blue painter's tape along the joints so you can see them easily. Chisel out the corners and cut away the tongue of the surrounding tiles if necessary. Apply glue to all four edges of the replacement tile.

REMOVING STAINS FROM LAMINATE TILE

STAIN	REMOVE WITH
Candle wax	Scrape carefully with plastic spatula
Crayon, rubber heel marks	Rub out with a dry cloth or acetone if needed
Grape juice or wine	Rub with a dry cloth or concentrated cleaner
Lipstick	Acetone or mineral spirits
Nail polish	Acetone-based nail polish remover
Paint or varnish	Wipe with water or mineral spirits while still wet; if dry, scrape carefully with a thin plastic spatula; if the stain still shows, rub with rubbing alcohol
Pen ink	Acetone or mineral spirits
Shoe polish	Acetone or mineral spirits
Tar	Acetone
Others	Start with concentrated cleaner, then acetone

After removing the stain, wipe the area with a damp cloth to remove residue.

REPAIRING A BLEMISH

1 How you cut out the damaged area depends on the pattern on the tile. If the tile is made with a wood-grain or other straight pattern, square the damaged area with a sharp utility knife. If the pattern is irregular, leave the outlines of the patch slightly irregular. Use a utility knife with a new blade but don't cut clear through all the layers of tile, only the top one. Use a vacuum to clean up the chips and dust.

2 Apply painter's tape around the damaged area. Squeeze out a dab of the manufacturer's repair compound into the damaged area and smooth it into the recess with the edge of a plastic spatula. The compound should be level with the masking tape (not the floor). Let the compound dry thoroughly.

3 When the compound has dried, remove the tape. Most compounds are made to shrink as they dry, so the repair should now be level with the surface.

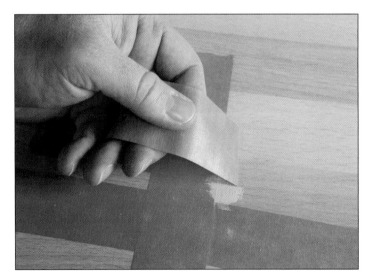

MAINTAINING PARQUET

Maintenance for a parquet floor depends somewhat on whether it's prefinished with either an acrylic or polyurethane finish. Some are no-wax finishes; others require waxing. Check with your tile retailer or manufacturer before buying cleaning products. Acrylic waxes are not usually recommended for wood floors, and some polyurethane finishes must not be waxed.

Most parquet or wood-floor cleaners have a solvent base, and some are more friendly to the environment than others. Water-base cleaners usually aren't recommended for parquet, but you can damp-mop the floor with an almost dry synthetic mop and water.

Wipe up spills immediately with a damp cloth and wipe the area dry with an old T-shirt or soft rag. Avoid cleaners that contain abrasives, caustic chemicals, bleach, or ammonia. For routine cleaning, use a solvent-base cleaner or a one-step cleaner/polish combination.

Regular vacuuming will help keep dirt and grit from scratching the floor and getting into joints. So will mats at entrances and casters or felt pads under furniture legs. Use rugs with a slip-resistant, but nonstaining, backing, and set mats in front of the kitchen sink and cooking areas to catch anything that might stain the tile.

Almost all wood finishes change color over time. Keeping the sunlight off the surface by closing the drapes will slow this process a little. The areas covered by rugs, however, will not change color, so you may end up with two wood tones over a long period of time.

One of the practical aspects of parquet is that you can refinish the entire floor when it shows wear. You can rent a pad sander and do the job yourself. Doing it yourself with a drum sander is not recommended. These heavy, powerful machines can quickly eat the top layer of wood off parquet; hire professional floor refinishers.

REPLACING PARQUET TILE

1 Use a circular saw with a fine-tooth blade to remove tiles. Set the cutting depth to the thickness of the tile. Make a series of parallel plunge cuts about 2 inches apart, stopping just short of the adjacent tiles.

2 Cut out the strips of the damaged tile with a ¾-inch or 1-inch chisel, keeping the chisel as flat as possible and the bevel down. Chisel the tongues off the adjacent tiles and scrape the old adhesive off the floor with a putty knife.

3 Remove the tongues on the replacement tile so it will slip into place. Clamp the tile to a work surface and cut the tongues with a handsaw.

4 Spread adhesive in the recess with a notched plastic scraper, and lower the replacement tile into it. Make sure the new tile is pressed flush with the old tile.

5 Clean off any adhesive that pushes up through the joints, and weight down the tile with heavy books or exercise weights. Let the adhesive dry overnight. If the replacement tile is prefinished, you can reduce the new-tile gloss with a light burnishing using #0000 steel wool. If the tile is unfinished, stain and finish it to match the surrounding floor.

MAINTAINING PARQUET

PROBLEM	REMEDY
Bubbles in finish	For light damage, sand and recoat; if heavy, sand, stain, and refinish
Chewing gum, crayon, candle wax	Freeze with ice in a bag, scrape with plastic scraper
Cigarette burns	Burnish with fine steel wool or scrape charred area; wax, or sand, stain, and refinish
Dents	Cover with dampened cloth and press with an electric iron
Scratches	Wax the area or hide the scratch with a thin coat of dusting spray rubbed into scratch
Seasonal cracks	Increase humidity in dry season–install humidifier, boil water, open dishwasher after rinse
Surface stains	Remove with sandpaper or steel wool, feathering edges; or clean specific stains with procedures and materials listed below
Heel marks	Wood cleaner or wax
Oil and grease	Try wood cleaner first; on waxed floor, use TSP or soap with high lye content; on surface finish, use TSP
Pet stains	Wood cleaner, followed by mild bleach or household vinegar for up to an hour; a remaining spot is not likely to sand out; cover damage with rug or remove, replace, and refinish
Ink	Use procedure for pet stains
Water spots	Buff lightly with #0000 steel wool, then wax; if necessary, sand with fine paper, stain, and recoat

MAINTAINING CARPET AND CORK TILE

Like any broadloom carpet, carpet tile will need periodic deep cleaning. You can rent machines for this purpose, but check the tile manufacturer's cleaning instructions to make sure you're using a product and method that will not weaken the adhesive bond. Some carpet tiles won't be affected by steam cleaning, but if you are unsure about yours, the safest product to use is a powder-base cleaner.

Be sure to vacuum first to remove as much loose dirt as possible. Move as much furniture out of the way as you can.

Most cork products are sealed with varnish that keeps dirt from clogging the pores of the cork. The varnish needs to be reapplied periodically, but many varnishes are not compatible with each other. Look up the manufacturer's instructions to decide which product to use.

You'll get more life out of your cork or carpet floor if you keep the grit from getting into the material in the first place. Put mats at entrances. Casters or cups under furniture legs will minimize dents. Floor mats can help prevent stains, and regular vacuuming helps keep tracked-in grit out of the fibers and joints.

CLEANING CARPET TILE

1 Consult the manufacturer or your retailer before buying a cleaning agent for carpet tile. If it's a cleaning powder, sprinkle it evenly across the floor. Properly applied, it should appear as a thin layer on the carpet.

2 Using a short-bristled floor brush, work the powder into the carpet fibers. Do not brush too heavily in any one area. Leave the powder in the fibers for the recommended time.

3 Vacuum the area with a vacuum that has beater bars. Work both with and against the grain to remove all the cleaning powder and soil.

FIXING CARPET SPROUTS

Sooner or later even the best carpet tile can sprout a loose fiber from the pile. Don't pull them out—you'll make holes. Instead, gently pull the sprouted fiber up and trim it flush with the others.

CLEANING CORK TILE

Vacuum cork tile with a canister vacuum and a floor brush rather than an upright vacuum or one with beater bars. The bars can damage the cork surface. Periodically damp-mop cork with a cotton string mop or synthetic sponge, being careful not to soak the surface. Cork finishes differ; use only the cleaning agent recommended specifically for your tile.

REPLACING CARPET AND CORK TILE

1 Using a metal straightedge (optional) and a sharp utility knife, make several passes in the center of the tile until you have cut through to the subfloor.

2 Insert a wide putty knife under the cut edge (not the joint) and pry up one-half of the tile, working the putty knife back and forth to break the adhesive bond. Working from the center to the edges, pry up the other half of the tile, replace the adhesive, press in the tile, and roll it with a floor roller.

CHAPTER HIGHLIGHTS

This chapter shows the tools you'll use for tiling. It also describes the basic steps in preparing for a tiling installation and installing the tile. Ceramic tile installation is the primary focus of this chapter. More information about installing other types of tile is shown with the tile projects in chapters 2, 3, 4, 5, and 6.

TILING TECHNIQUES

Learning by repetition is the key to developing the skills for a successful tile installation. If you're new to tiling or just a little unsure of the process, rehearse your skills with a practice surface–a couple of sheets of ½-inch backerboard. Even thinner ¼-inch stock will do, although you'll have to anchor it to keep it from moving around. Mix up a small batch of thinset, spread it, comb it, then scrape it off and try again. Most thinsets have a reasonably long open time, which will allow you to reuse your practice batch until you get the ridges right. You also can use the practice surface to learn laying the tile in with a slight twist before the mortar sets up. Line up a carpenter's level on the edges of the tile to get the feel of what it takes to nudge them into line–especially when you're getting close to when the mortar cures. Then let the mortar dry and try your hand at

grouting. The two most important aspects are packing the joints with enough grout and cleaning off the excess at the right time. It is better to have some experience with these skills, described in previous chapters, before starting the real tiling project.

Then you need to think about organization. Plan your work in sections. When preparing the room, start with the easier tasks–remove the trim first, then the appliances. Bring all the tools to the work area to eliminate repeated trips to the basement, garage, or hardware store. Lay all the field tiles the first day. Come back the next day to lay the cut tiles on the edges so you won't have to walk on freshly laid tile and risk dislodging some tiles. Think through the installation steps before you start–and take breaks from the work to keep yourself fresh.

CHOOSING TOOLS

If you're like most homeowners, you probably already own at least a few of the tools you need for a tiling project. Tools commonly considered carpentry tools are used mostly to demolish and prepare for tile installation. Although many of these tools have many uses, their application to tiling is limited to specific tasks. Whatever your project, you can't expect to accomplish these tasks without the right tools.

A **16-ounce framing hammer** is essential—heavy enough to drive framing nails or to shore up a floor, yet light enough for trim work. In a tiling project, you'll use a ⅜-or ½-inch **cordless drill** primarily to drive backerboard screws and fasten battens to walls. You'll also need one if you're framing a custom shower pan or drilling holes for pipes in backerboard. A cordless model keeps the workplace free of extension cords. Buy a **hole saw** to cut holes in backerboard larger than 1 inch.

A **stud finder** will find studs in the walls and joists in the floor, allowing you to position underlayment and backerboard correctly. Get an electronic one that locates the framing by sensing density, not nails.

You might think a **reciprocating saw** is made only for heavy-duty demolition, but if you're installing a new countertop base, it makes quick work of cutting the fasteners in an old one.

For pulling nails when tearing up underlayment, nothing beats a **cat's paw**. You might also need a **flat pry bar** and a **ripping bar** to pry up the old plywood.

You'll need a **small sledge** and a **cold chisel** to tear out old tile on a floor or wall. Smoothing high spots on a wood subfloor is a snap with a **belt sander**. Use a **grinder** with a masonry abrasive wheel to knock down high spots on a slab.

A full-size or close-work **hacksaw** will cut steel and copper pipes as well as the rusted anchor bolts on a toilet. A **utility knife** does everything from sharpening pencils to cutting drywall and resilient, carpet, and cork tile. Keep plenty of blades on hand and change them often so you're always cutting with a sharp one. **Wire cutters** often come in handy.

Use a **circular saw** to cut framing for a shower stall and to remove wood floors. For quick work, a **toolbox saw** packs a lot of cutting power into a compact size. Cut countertop holes for sinks with a **jigsaw**.

An **adjustable wrench** will loosen fixture fasteners and fittings—one size fits all. To loosen large compression or slip fittings, **groove-joint pliers** will give you the right amount of leverage. And for a tight grip on stop-valve nuts, use a **combination wrench**—one end is open and the other is closed or box-end.

You'll need a variety of **screwdrivers**, both phillips and straight, to remove faucets and handles, as well as to pry up the corner of the carpet you're removing. You'll need stiff **putty knives** to scrape up old adhesive, but you'll need a **razor scraper** to take up resilient flooring.

TOOLS FOR DEMOLITION AND PREPARATION

Carpenter's hammer

Small sledge

Utility knife

Putty knives

Razor scraper

Hole saw

Jigsaw

Toolbox saw

Hacksaw

Cold chisel

Circular saw

Angle grinder with coarse masonry disc

Reciprocating saw

Adjustable wrench

Wire cutters

Cordless drill

Stud finder

Groove-joint pliers

Screwdrivers

Cat's paw

Belt sander

Combination wrenches

Pry bar

TOOLS FOR TILE

To demolish and prepare for a tiling project, a traditional array of carpentry tools will come in handy. When you actually install and grout the tile, however, you'll need specialized tools, along with some standard hand tools.

Use a **carpenter's level** as a straightedge to line up tiles in a row and to check the surface for tiles that are higher or lower than the rest. A **tape measure** is a convenient, compact rule for all measuring tasks, and is especially necessary when you're laying out the job. Make sure you have a 25-foot tape with a 1-inch blade. You'll need that length to reach across rooms, and the wide blade won't buckle when you extend it.

Backerboard is made from cement and fiberglass mesh. It's tough and won't cut easily without a **carbide backerboard scriber**. You'll also need a **drywall corner knife** to tape backerboard in corners. Smooth the cut edges of backerboard with a **contour plane** and round off cut tiles with a **masonry stone**.

You must have a **chalk line** for a tiling project, so you can extend layout lines from marks to both walls and keep tile rows parallel to each other.

To mix thinset mortar, use a **heavy-duty drill** that has a **mixing paddle**. Rent one if you don't own one and won't need one much in the future.

Different jobs and different mortars require different **trowels**, and you'll need a **grout float** to fill the joints properly. You'll need a **rubber mallet** to level tiles with a **beater block** and a **tile sponge** to clean the grout from the surface of the tiles.

Cutting a few tiles is easy with a **snap cutter** but for large jobs, rent a **wet saw**. Use **tile nippers** to chip away small sections of tile when you're making round cuts.

A **margin trowel** will get mortar into tight spaces and is a handy tool for scooping mortar from a bucket or other mixing container.

Then for finishing off the installation of resilient flooring, rent a **floor roller**.

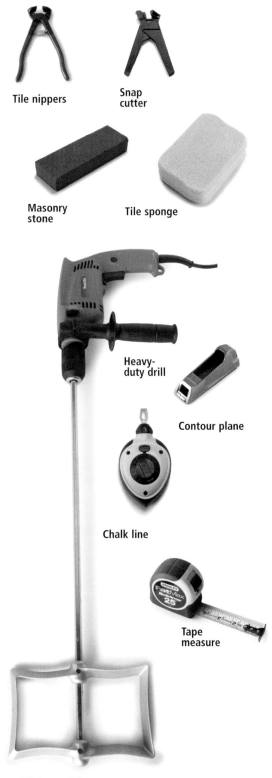

Tile nippers

Snap cutter

Masonry stone

Tile sponge

Heavy-duty drill

Contour plane

Chalk line

Tape measure

Mixing paddle

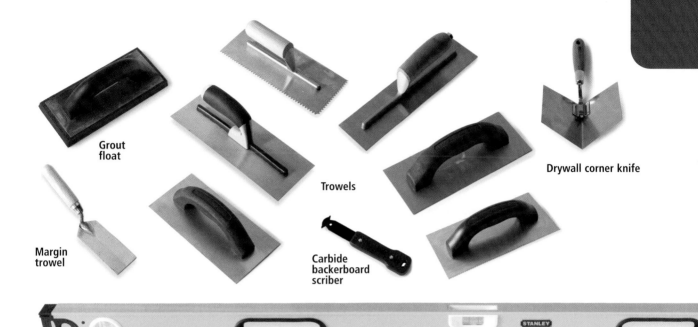

Grout
float

Trowels

Drywall corner knife

Margin
trowel

Carbide
backerboard
scriber

Carpenter's level

Rubber mallet

Beater block

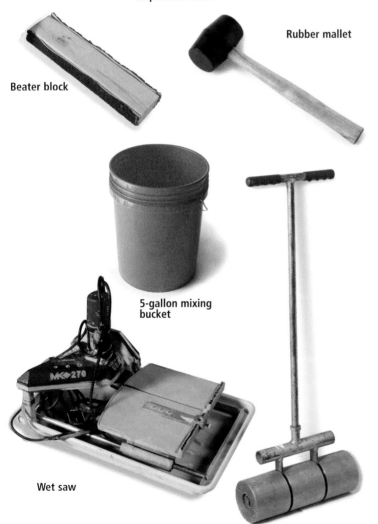

5-gallon mixing
bucket

Wet saw

100-pound floor roller

WHAT TO RENT?

If you only have some of the tools needed for tiling projects, you may want to buy the smaller ones and rent larger tools that you would use rarely, such as a snap cutter, a wet saw, a 100-lb. floor roller, or a heavy-duty mixing drill.

Think twice about other power tools, however. If you don't have a circular saw, for example, this might be a good reason to purchase one. If you're already committed to a do-it-yourself tiling project, you'll probably need a circular saw later. The same is true of a jigsaw and even a reciprocating saw. Buy the best you can afford. When renting, don't reserve all the tools at once. For example, you won't need the floor roller to roll resilient tile until you've laid it, and then only for a day.

REMOVING BASEBOARDS, THRESHOLDS, & APPLIANCES

The first step with any tile installation is removal of moldings, thresholds, furniture, appliances, and fixtures in the tiling area. Remove everything you can so the surface will be easier to prepare and so the entire surface will be easier to tile.

Move the appliances out of the way as soon as possible, but remember that ceramic tile and stone will raise the height of the floor–and reduce the opening height for undercounter appliances. So before you move the appliances, mark the countertops where you'll need to shim them or mark openings you'll need to enlarge to accommodate the new height. Resilient tile won't raise appliances much, but ceramic tile will–by the thickness of new underlayment plus backerboard and tile. You may also have to relocate water, gas, and electric lines.

Most baseboards have a shoe molding, also called quarter round. Take the shoe molding off first; cut the paint line at the top of the baseboard with a utility knife so you're less likely to chip the paint when you pull the baseboard away.

PREPARING THE ROOM

Removing fixtures and moldings is only the first preparation step. You will also need to protect other surfaces in the room and keep construction debris and dust from migrating into the rest of the house.

If you're tiling only the walls, protect the floor with a tarp— reinforced plastic tarps are cheap and will have many uses later on. Outside the work site, lay tarps in hallways and place a small rug or doormat just outside the door.

Old sheets will keep the dust out of built-in cabinets and bookshelves, but you should move furniture to another room.

Tape cardboard over ductwork openings and registers, and hang plastic in open entries. Put an exhaust fan in a window— blowing outside—to increase ventilation.

REMOVING BASEBOARDS

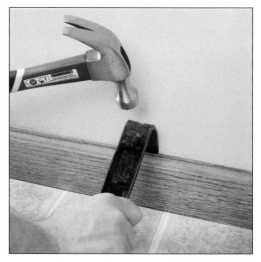

Starting at the nail nearest a corner or joint, work a small pry bar between the baseboard and the wall to loosen the nail. You can insert a wide putty knife between the pry bar and the wall to protect the wall. Loosen all the nails before removing a baseboard section.

REMOVING A TILE BORDER

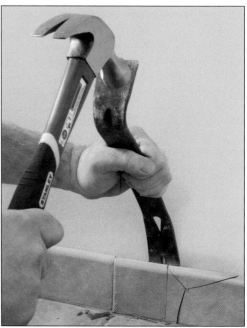

Tap a pry bar behind each tile and pop it off the wall. If necessary, you can protect the wall with a piece of scrap inserted behind the bar. Scrape off adhesive with a stiff putty knife.

REMOVING VINYL MOLDING

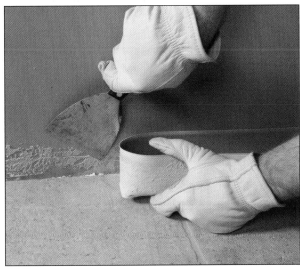

Push a wide putty knife behind the top corner of a joint in the molding and pry the molding off the wall. Scrape off the adhesive, keeping the knife flat against the wall to minimize gouging—multiple passes work better than removing the adhesive all at once.

REMOVING THRESHOLDS

Cut through the threshold to the floor with a handsaw or backsaw. Remove each section of the threshold with a pry bar. For thresholds fastened with screws, remove the screws, then slide the threshold out from under the trim.

REMOVING A DISHWASHER

Open the dishwasher and remove the mounting screws from the flange, then close the door and lock it. Grasp the sides of the door and slide the unit forward, lifting it up and rocking it from side to side. Get someone to help push the supply and drain lines through the cabinet holes as you pull.

REMOVING A STOVE TOP

Turn off the gas or electricity to the stove and disconnect the gas flex line or electric cable. Working below the cabinet, remove the mounting clips. Push the unit up from below with one hand while you slide a piece of scrap under the lip of the stove top with your other hand. Lift the unit up and out.

USING A DOLLY

You can slide heavy appliances across the floor, but an appliance dolly makes the job easy and safe. Slide the dolly plate under the appliance, tighten the strap, tip the unit back and release the support carriage, and roll it away.

REMOVING TOILETS AND SINKS

You might be tempted to leave the toilet and sink in place and tile around them when tiling a bathroom. It's better to resist the temptation, however. Tiling the floor will be a lot easier and will go more quickly with the fixtures out of the way. A clear floor space allows you to lay out the tile installation precisely, snap chalk lines wherever you need them, and set the tiles without the annoyance of working around and bumping into stationary objects. Besides, if you leave the fixtures in place, you'll have to cut tiles to fit around them—a difficult and time-consuming task. It's almost impossible to keep the edges of cut tile from looking ragged.

The first step in removing a toilet or sink is to turn the water off. If your fixtures have stop valves, shut them off, being careful not to turn the valve handle too tightly. If the supply line leaks after you've shut the valve off, replace the valve.

If you don't have stop valves, shut the water off at the main valve that supplies the house. Then install stop valves before you remove the toilet and sink so you won't have to leave water off to the rest of the house while you're working on the bathroom.

Once the water is off, flush the toilet and open the faucets to drain as much water as you can from the fixture. Then unhook the supply lines, either at the valve or from the fixture.

Because it's impossible to completely drain the fixtures and the supply lines, removing them is bound to spill some water on the floor. Keep a pile of rags or old towels handy (towels are better) to wipe it up.

You can lay new tile over the old if you're sure that your floor will support the additional weight. You'll also need to cut the door and the trim, and install a taller threshold or some other transition to make room for the rise in the floor height.

REMOVING A TOILET

1 Shut off the water by closing the supply-line valve. Then flush the toilet to empty the tank. Push the water from the bowl with a plunger, then pry or pull off the anchor-bolt caps. Remove the nut on the anchor bolts with an adjustable wrench or groove-joint pliers. Cut through stubborn bolts and nuts with a hacksaw.

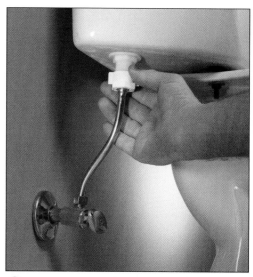

2 Loosen the supply-line compression nut and pull the line out of the valve. Rock the toilet back and forth to break the seal of the wax ring from the closet flange in the floor, then lift the toilet from the floor. If the toilet is heavy, remove the tank before carrying the unit to another room. Pull the wax ring out of the flange and dispose of it. Stuff a large rag into the open drain to keep out debris.

REMOVING A SINK

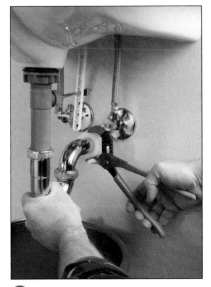

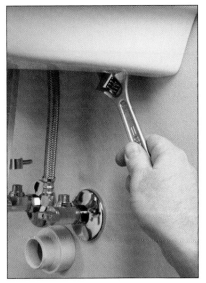

1 Shut off both the hot- and cold-water stop valves. Loosen the supply-line compression nuts with an adjustable wrench, then pull the line from the valve. Place a bucket or pile of rags under the trap to catch any water released when you remove it. Loosen the slip-nut fitting on both ends of the trap with a groove-joint pliers and pull the trap from the tailpiece. Pour the trap water in a bucket.

2 Using an adjustable or open-end wrench, loosen the sink mounting bolts. Do not remove the bolts or nuts completely yet.

3 If your sink has legs under the front edge, remove them. Then hold the sink with both hands and pull it straight up and off the mounting brackets. Remove the brackets from the wall.

▶ Almost all sinks, both wall-mounted and pedestal units, are mounted in essentially the same way. The rear sink flange hooks down into a bracket fastened to the studs or blocking with large screws. There are different types of brackets, and some are two-piece constructions. Front legs or a pedestal may also be installed to help support the sink and add to its style. Working from below, you'll find some sort of bolted bracket that attaches a pedestal or legs to the sink. An adjustable or box-end wrench will usually remove them. It helps to apply a little penetrating oil before you start work to loosen fasteners that are frozen.

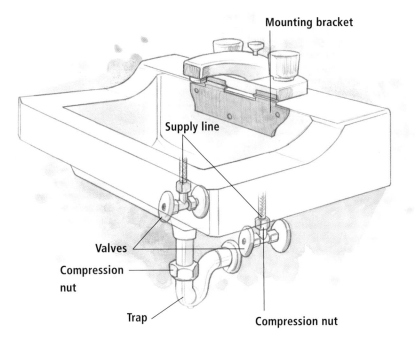

Mounting bracket

Supply line

Valves

Compression nut

Trap

Compression nut

Preparing Floors and Walls for Tile

Tile substrates must be smooth and flat, and walls should be as plumb as possible. Floors are usually easier to prepare if you first remove the existing flooring so you can look for damage hidden under the finished flooring. With the flooring removed, you won't have to cut doors to clear the raised surface of the floor. Remove wallpaper or paneling from walls and degloss painted surfaces, but don't strip the paint. Stripping can leave a residue that weakens the mortar bond.

Concrete slabs require extra care. Stop water from wicking into the mortar with a waterproofing membrane and cover cracks with an isolation membrane that rolls on as a liquid (see *page 125*). (Apply an all-in-one membrane to fix both problems.) Push on the wall and screw soft spots to the studs. You can tile over existing wall tile, but it's safer to remove it. Remove all existing tile on walls in wet locations, such as baths.

REMOVING RESILIENT FLOORING

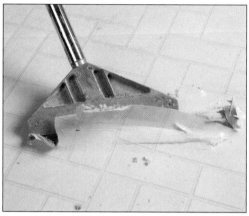

Cut the sheet into 15-inch strips with a utility knife. Starting at one of your cut lines, pry up the sheet with a scraper, rolling the strip as you go. For unbacked resilients, you can soften the adhesive with a hair dryer. Spray the remaining adhesive with adhesive remover. Then use a scraper to peel the residue from the floor.

REMOVING CARPET

Remove all thresholds and transitions, then cut the carpet and pad into 15-inch-wide strips. Pry up a corner of the carpet with a pry bar and pull up the corner with pliers. Pull up the carpet, rolling the strips as you go. Then grasp each strip of pad with both hands and pull it from the floor. Remove the tack strips with a pry bar. Wear gloves to remove the tack strips—the tacks are sharp.

REMOVING OLD TILE

Crack the center of a tile with a small sledge and cold chisel. Break out the tile with the sledge and brush loose pieces out of the way. Tap a wide cold chisel or brickset under the edge of the adjoining tiles and pop them off. Scrape the adhesive from the underlayment.

MARKING DEFECTS

Working in sections, set a 4-foot level on the wall and floor; mark high spots, depressions, and other defects that could prevent the tile from properly adhering. Check the wall for plumb at the corners, and mark both ends of any area that will need leveling.

LEVELING LOW SPOTS AND HIGH SPOTS

1 Vacuum the floor, then trowel thinset into depressions with a mason's trowel. Feather out the edges of the thinset level with the floor. When the mortar is dry, sand the edges to feather them, if necessary.

2 Set the heads of all nails and screws below the surface. Then use a belt sander to level the high spots you marked.

LEVELING THE WALL

Skim-coat a layer of thinset on any walls that are out of plumb and fill depressions. If installing backerboard on studs, mark stud centers on the edge of the ceiling. Cut and fasten backerboard, centering its edges on the studs. Place the backerboard so you can cut—and waste—as little as possible.

INSTALLING UNDERLAYMENT

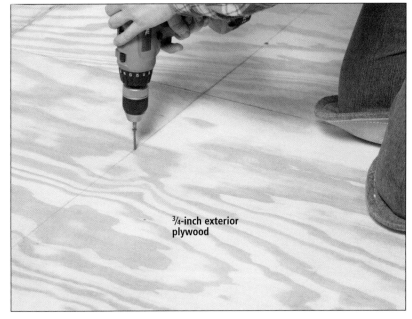

¾-inch exterior plywood

If your subfloor has deteriorated, you'll need new underlayment. You can install new material over the old, but it is usually best to keep the new floor level as close as possible to the old by tearing up the existing material and installing new plywood over the joists.

Apply construction adhesive to the joists and start with a full sheet squared to a corner. Center the plywood edge on the joists and drive screws into the joists. Lay half sheets next to full sheets to offset the joints. Use 8d nails as spacers between the sheets and leave ¼-inch space at the walls.

INSTALLING A NEW COUNTERTOP BASE

The first step when tiling a countertop is removing the old countertop and building a new base.

Laminate and wood countertops are easy to remove with a pry bar and some effort. Taking off ceramic tile is somewhat more tedious—and a lot more messy. But removing the old surface is the best way to make sure the job is done correctly and looks like a professional installation. Tiling over an existing counter can raise it by an inch or more; and while that may seem insignificant, it can make it uncomfortable to use the kitchen or bath. Also, if you install a new base, you won't have to cut tiles to fit over the existing backsplash.

You can leave the sink in place or take it out before prying up the counter. Removing the sink will lighten the load, of course.

Cut a new base from ¾-inch exterior-grade plywood. It's made with moisture-resistant glues and is commonly sold in 4×8-foot sheets. Add bracing under any joints and on the front and back of appliance openings wider than 3 feet.

Standard depth for countertops is 24 inches front-to-back, including a ½- to ¾-inch overhang. No wall is perfectly flat, so you'll need to cut the sheet a little deeper than 24 inches so you can scribe and cut it to fit the wall. If your plans include a drop-in range, cut the hole for it as you would a sink.

REMOVING AN OLD COUNTERTOP

1 Using a screwdriver or cordless drill, remove the screws that fasten the countertop to the cleats or corner blocks. Do not loosen the fasteners that attach corner blocks to the cabinet frame.

2 Push a pry bar into the joint between the countertop and cabinet, then pry up the countertop. Lift the countertop and carry it to another room. Cut heavy countertops into sections with a reciprocating saw for easier removal.

BUILDING A NEW COUNTERTOP BASE

Cut a piece of ¾-inch exterior-grade plywood to the dimensions of the cabinet— plus ½ to ¾ inch for an overhang. Set the plywood on the cabinet and attach it to the frame with 2-inch coated screws.

CUTTING THE SINK HOLE

1 Use the manufacturer's template to mark the dimensions of the cutout, or set the sink upside down on the plywood and trace its outline. Remove the sink and draw parallel lines that measure the width of the flange inside the outline.

2 Drill a starter hole for the jigsaw blade and cut along the interior line. When you approach the final turn, have someone help support the cutout from below so the saw blade won't bind. After you have cut the hole, install a waterproofing membrane.

TYPICAL TILED COUNTERTOP CONSTRUCTION

Bullnose tile

Tile

Thinset

Bullnose edge tile

1× build-up strip

Plywood

Backerboard

Cabinet

1× or ¾" plywood cleat

▲ The weight of ceramic tile and backerboard needs adequate support. Both new and existing kitchen and vanity cabinets should be reinforced with 1× frame supports around the top of the perimeter. Install the cleats first, then the plywood and backerboard. Attach build-up strips to support the edge tiles.

INSTALLING BACKERBOARD

Installing cement backerboard requires about the same skills as those used for drywall. But even if you're new to remodeling, you'll find backerboard goes on easily.

Like drywall, backerboard joints need to be centered on the joists or studs, so you'll have to mark the location of the joists on the walls and the studs on the edge of the ceiling to guide you. On a floor, look for the fastener lines in the underlayment–that's where the joists are. On a wall, the fastener lines may be obscured by joint compound and paint, so locate the studs with an electric stud finder.

Offset the backerboard joints by a half sheet where possible to increase the strength of the substrate. Tape the joints with gummed tape. You can use paper tape, but gummed tape goes on in about one-third the time and is well worth its slight additional cost. Four-inch tape will make a stronger joint than two-inch tape.

CUTTING BACKERBOARD

1 Protect finished flooring surfaces with a tarp. Set a drywall square at the position of the cut; with firm pressure, scribe the line with a carbide scriber. You don't have to cut through the board.

2 Stand the sheet on edge with the side opposite the scored line facing you. Hold the sheet on both sides, put your knee behind the scribed line, and snap the board toward you.

3 Keep the sheet at the same angle and cut through the unscored side with a utility knife. Make several passes with the knife to separate the pieces.

CUTTING SMALL HOLES

4 Smooth the cut edge of the backerboard with a contour plane or masonry stone. Whatever tool you use, keep it perpendicular to the edge of the board. Make several passes until the edge is flat.

Set the backerboard edge against the pipe (inset) and mark the position and diameter of the hole. Place the drill point of a hole saw on the center mark you made; use light pressure and high speed to cut through the backerboard.

CUTTING LARGE HOLES

1 Measure the width of the obstruction and draw a circle that size on the backerboard with a compass. Then score completely through the backerboard mesh with a carbide scriber.

2 Tap around the scored edge with a hammer, supporting the cutout on the other side. Keep tapping until the backerboard crumbles around the circumference.

3 Cut through the mesh on the opposite side with a utility knife. Push out the cutout and smooth the edges with a contour plane or masonry stone.

INSTALLING BACKERBOARD ON FLOORS

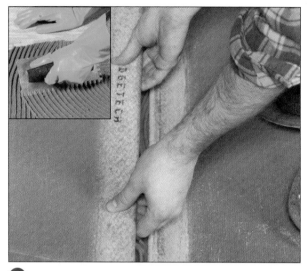

1 Mix thinset mortar in a clean 5-gallon bucket or other suitable container and pour a small amount on the underlayment. Using the smooth edge of a notched trowel, spread the mortar in a thick, even coat. Then switch to the notched edge of the trowel and comb the mortar into ridges, holding the trowel at a 45-degree angle. Center the edge of the first sheet of backerboard on a joist, then lower the board into the mortar.

2 Using a drill/driver, drive backerboard screws about every 8 inches. Use 2-inch screws at the joists and 1¼-inch screws in the field. Drive the screwheads flush. Lay each remaining sheet in the mortar with offset joints and a ⅛-inch gap between them—¼ inch at walls. Walk on the boards to set them in the mortar.

3 Seal the joints with 2- or 4-inch pregummed fiberglass tape, pressing the tape onto the backerboard. (See "Tape Tips," *opposite page*).

4 To finish the joint, apply a thin coat of thinset over the tape with a margin trowel or mason's trowel. Completely fill the recess on both sides of the joint with mortar, then feather out the edges to eliminate high spots that could cause the tile to crack.

INSTALLING BACKERBOARD ON WALLS

1 Nail blocking between the studs to support horizontal seams if the studs are more than 16 inches on center. Apply construction adhesive to the studs and fasten the boards with backerboard screws. Rest the next sheets on 8d nails to make a ⅛-inch gap between the sheets.

2 Tape each joint with 2- or 4-inch gummed mesh tape, unrolling the tape as you go. Cut the tape at the end of the joint with a utility knife.

3 Trowel the taped joint with a thin coat of thinset. Fill the recess at the joint and level it with the backerboard. Feather the edges smooth.

TAPE TIPS

Gummed fiberglass mesh tape is easier to use for taping backerboard joints and it's stronger, but you can also use ungummed paper tape.

Do not precut the tape to length—precut lengths may stick to themselves before you can stick them onto the board. Instead, unroll the tape as you press it into the joint, then cut it when you reach the end of the joint.

When taping a corner with 2-inch tape, run one length along one edge of the corner and another length along the other edge. Bridge the two edges with a third length of tape.

Four-inch tape makes quick work of taping corners. Fold the tape in half as you press it into the corner.

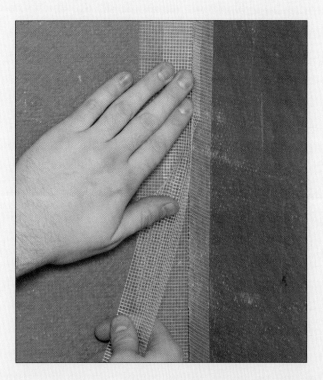

MARKING LAYOUT LINES

Layout lines can make all the difference between a professional-looking surface and a sloppy installation. They keep your tile square to the room and evenly spaced.

You can use your layout sketch to find the point to snap the first line, but it's better to dry-lay one spaced row of tile in both directions. Mark the edge of a tile about 2 feet from a wall, then snap the line parallel to your center chalk lines.

You can establish grids to organize your work in sections. A grid outlines a group of layout lines and defines a small area in which you'll spread mortar and lay tile before moving

MARKING LAYOUT LINES ON FLOORS

1 Snap chalk lines and square them with a 3-4-5 triangle (see illustration, *below*). Dry-lay tiles and spacers on each line and adjust the layout until the edge tiles are the same width. Mark the floor several feet from one wall where a grout joint falls, then extend this mark to both walls—parallel to your squared lines.

2 Snap a chalk line at the point you have marked. Measure from this line distances equal to an even number of tiles and grout joints; snap layout lines at these points. Repeat the process along the other axis.

SQUARING THE LAYOUT

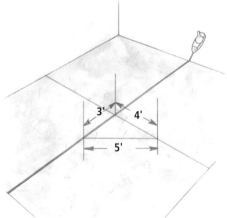

Snap perpendicular lines at the midpoints of the walls. To square the lines, mark 3 feet from the center along one leg and 4 feet on the other. If the diagonal distance between the marks is 5 feet, the lines are square.

GETTING THE EDGE TILES EVEN

Dry-lay tile in both directions, then adjust the layout until you have spaces for tiles of equal width at both edges.

on to the next section. How large a grid should be will depend on how complicated your layout is, how quickly the mortar sets up, your skill level, and the size of the tile.

To start, set a grid of about 2-foot squares. Measure from the reference lines in both directions by an amount that equals several tiles plus grout joints, then snap lines at these points.

MARKING LAYOUT LINES ON WALLS

1 Set a carpenter's level on the wall at least 2 feet from a corner and where a grout line will fall. Pencil a line along the edge of the level and extend it to the floor and ceiling with a chalk line.

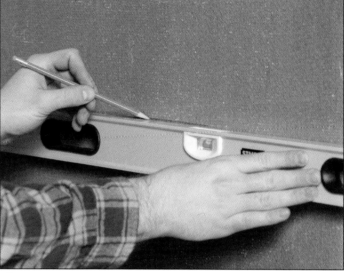

2 Set the level perpendicular to the vertical chalk line, about midway up the wall—where a grout line will fall. Pencil a line along the level and extend it to both walls with a chalk line. Mark the wall at intervals equal to the dimensions of the tile and a grout joint, then snap layout lines at your marks.

DRAW PLENTY OF LINES

Decorative tiles and borders and different-shape rooms add to the complexity of a layout, but you can simplify the job by snapping plenty of layout lines. Once you have snapped the major layout sections, mark the position of decorative tiles or borders. Snap a line on both axes at each point the pattern or the tile size changes.

Rectangular Room

L-Shape Room

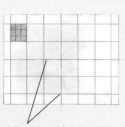

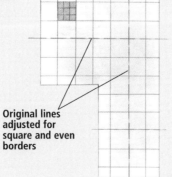

Diagonal Layout

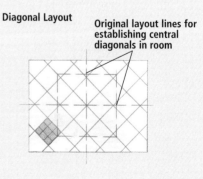

Original layout lines for establishing central diagonals in room

Original lines adjusted for square and even borders

Original lines at midpoints of walls adjusted for square and even borders

INSTALLING RADIANT HEAT

R adiant floor heating used to be expensive and complicated to install. Electrical heating mats have put this comfort within the reach of most homeowners. You don't need to be an expert in heating systems or electrical work—just have a few skills and a little common sense—to install above-floor mats.

Radiant heat has some advantages over other heating systems. Forced-air heating systems, for example, create different temperatures at different elevations in a room. If you're uncomfortable in one part of a room, you can turn up the heat, making another part of the room too hot and increasing your heating costs. Radiant heating does not discriminate—it warms the entire area consistently. And, it doesn't make noise or stir up dust. You can regulate the heat in each room by installing separate thermostats.

Heating mats keep cold tile floors comfortably warm. Ceramic and stone are excellent conductors of heat; of all tile materials, they will transfer the heat quickly, making your system run more efficiently. Parquet and laminate tile are also efficient heat conductors. Vinyl tile is also a good choice but should not be heated above 85 degrees. Carpet tile acts as insulation and won't distribute heat as well as solid materials.

Before you install the mats, sketch their location carefully. You won't need them under closets, appliances, or sinks and vanities.

Put thermostats on interior walls so they won't be triggered by the lower temperature of an outside wall. You won't need a large system in a small room, and the lower current drain of a smaller system may allow you to tap power from a nearby outlet. However, you should install a separate circuit for the mats wherever possible.

1 Mark the location of the thermostat on the wall, then install a junction box 60 inches above the floor. Add a new circuit or extend an existing one with 12/2 cable, but don't connect the circuit at the service panel. Roll out the heating mat, keeping it about 3 inches from the walls and fixtures. Staple the mat to the subfloor or tack it with double-sided tape.

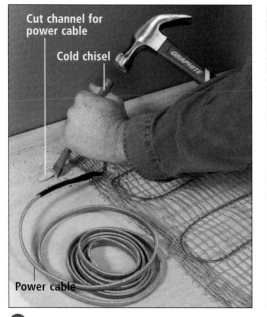

Cut channel for
power cable

Cold chisel

Power cable

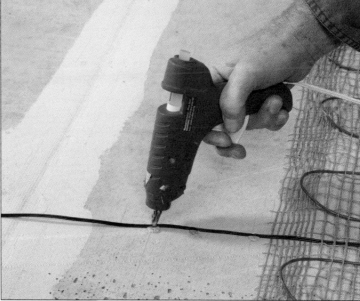

2 Some mats come with ribboned power leads that will lie flat on the subfloor, but if your power lead is thicker than the mat, cut a channel in the backerboard with a cold chisel. Dab hot glue in the channel and press the power lead into it. Set surface-mounted leads into beads of hot glue. Make sure the leads don't cross each other or run perpendicular across a heating element.

3 If your system has a sensor bulb, weave it between two heating elements and keep it in place with hot glue. Follow the manufacturer's instructions to check the mat for conductivity.

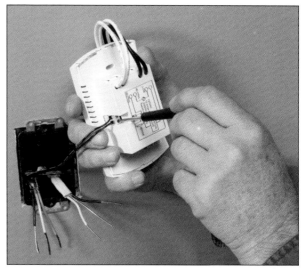

4 Working in sections, spread thinset over the mat with the flat side of a ³⁄₈-inch notched trowel (see *page 165*). Then comb the mortar to a uniform ¹⁄₄-inch depth, working slowly to avoid snagging the mat. Tile the mortared section and repeat the process until the entire floor is tiled.

5 Following the manufacturer's diagrams and instructions, attach the two sensor wires to the terminals in the thermostat. Connect the ground wire from the mat directly to the house ground. Wire the rest of the connections following the manufacturer's instructions. Then connect the new circuit at the service panel.

INSTALLING CERAMIC TILE

Before you start any ceramic tile installation, make sure you level depressions, reduce high spots, plumb the walls, and perform other preparation steps as shown on *pages 148–153*. Then install backerboard, if necessary (see *pages 156–159*). You won't need backerboard on a slab floor or on drywall or plaster where moisture doesn't collect, but you will need backerboard on wood surfaces or any wall or floor that gets wet. Consider using backerboard even on surfaces that don't need it. Backerboard provides a smooth, solid substrate for ceramic tile and stone when properly installed. After you have fastened and taped the backerboard, let the joints dry and then vacuum it with a canister vacuum and a brush to remove residual cement dust.

Because the color of ceramic tile can vary from dye lot to dye lot–and even within lots–go through each carton and make sure the color is consistent throughout the tile. If you're laying saltillo or other handmade tile, the color differences won't matter as much–it's part of the charm of the material. Mix handmade tiles from each box to distribute any color variations randomly throughout the installation. Set chipped or damaged pieces aside and use them when you cut tile for the edges.

1 Pour enough mortar to cover a layout section. Spread the mortar evenly, but do not cover your layout lines. Then comb the thinset with the notched edge of 45-degree angle.

TILE PATTERNS

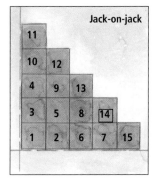

A jack-on-jack pattern is the easiest pattern to set. Lay the first tile at the intersection of your layout lines, then set the remaining tiles as shown above.

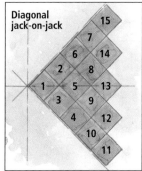

Diagonal patterns always require cut edge tiles. Dry-lay the pattern carefully to make sure these edge tiles will be as close to a full diagonal as possible.

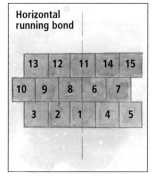

Horizontal running bond requires you to mark the exact center of the first tile and lay it on one axis. Work from that tile to both sides, then start the next row on the center mark.

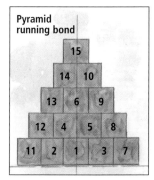

A pyramid running bond stacks the centers of tiles not only on alternate rows but also on both sides of the center axis. Mark all the center tiles before you lay this pattern.

Organize the installation: Figure out how many tiles you'll need in each layout section and stack tiles at strategic points throughout the room. Having the tile ready to install will save you time when you're ready to start a new section.

Start mixing thinset by pouring water in a clean 5-gallon bucket or a plastic utility tub. Add about half the dry thinset and mix it with a ½-inch drill equipped with a mortar-mixing paddle. Keep the speed low and keep the paddle in the mix to avoid adding air. Once the first half of the mortar is mixed thoroughly, add mortar a little at a time and continue mixing. Let the mix set (slake) for 10 minutes before you trowel it on.

Applying thinset properly takes some practice. You need to form ridges about the depth of the trowel notches that compress and cover the entire back of the tile when you lay it. Be sure to follow the manufacturer's directions for mixing water and dry mortar. Thinset will not hold ridges if it's too wet. If it's too dry, it will not compress and will adhere poorly to the tile. Test your mixture every now and then (at least once in a layout section) by pulling up a tile and examining the back. You're mixing it correctly if the thinset completely covers the surface.

Space loose tiles with plastic spacers, available from tile retailers and home centers. You won't need spacers when laying lugged tile or sheet-mounted tile. Lay spacers flat at corners to space four tiles evenly. Set the rest of the spacers vertically so they will be easier to remove.

Whenever possible, lay the field tiles first and let the mortar dry. Then cut and install all the edge tiles at the same time.

2 Set the first tile at the intersection of your layout lines, twisting slightly to help embed it in the mortar. Keep the edges of the tile on the layout lines.

3 Using the layout pattern you have chosen (see illustration, *opposite),* lay the next tile on the layout line with the same twisting motion. Set spacers upright between the tiles and snug the tiles against the spacers.

4 Continue laying tiles along both legs of your layout lines using your pattern as a guide and spacing the tiles with upright spacers.

5 After laying three or four tiles, set a carpenter's level against their edges to make sure the tiles are lined up correctly. Scrape off any excess thinset from the layout lines. Adjust the tiles if necessary.

6 Continue laying the tiles and setting spacers, filling in the quadrant between the layout lines. If you need to straighten or reset a tile, support your weight on a 2-foot square of ¾-inch plywood. Use two plywood squares so you can move one while kneeling on the other.

7 At each corner, turn the upright spacers flat side down and snug the corners of the tile against the spacers.

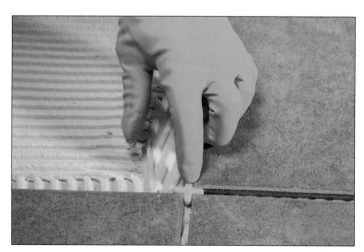

8 When you have completed one section, use a carpenter's level again to check for tiles that are higher or lower than the rest of the surface. Tack a scrap piece of carpet to a 12- to 15-inch 2×4 to make a beater block. Tap high tiles in place using the beater block and a rubber mallet.

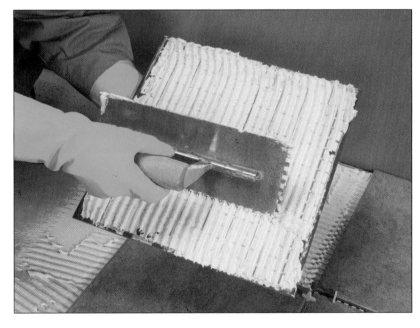

9 If you find a tile that's lower than the others, pry it up with the point of a utility knife and spread more thinset on the back of the tile. Reset the tile in place and level it with the beater block. Clean excess mortar out of the joints by dragging a spacer along the joint. Remove loose bits of mortar and let the thinset cure overnight.

Cutting Ceramic Tile

deally the dimensions of your installation would correspond exactly to a multiple of your tile dimensions so you wouldn't have to cut tiles for the edges. However, most projects require tiles to be cut for the edges and corners of a layout and where pipes come through the floor or wall, or around doors, windows, or other openings.

If you've never cut tile before, take a few practice cuts first so you'll avoid errors that could increase your installation time.

After you have laid the field tile and let the mortar dry, you can measure the width of the edge tiles. Walls are rarely uniform, so edge tiles rarely can be the same size around the perimeter of the room. If they are, however, or if they don't vary by more than 1/8 inch, cut all of them the same size, trowel on the adhesive, and lay the tiles. Small variations along the edge can be covered by the baseboard or molding. If the tiles vary in width by more than 1/8 inch, cut each one separately. Cut all the tiles and lay them in order before spreading mortar and setting the tiles so you won't be in danger of working longer than the thinset's setting time.

For just a few cuts, you'll only need tile nippers or a rod saw with a carbide blade. Rent a snap cutter to make quick work of cutting thin tile, or a wet saw to cut thicker tiles or a large quantity of them. Cut tile edges are rough. Either hide them under toe-kicks or smooth them with a masonry stone.

MARKING STRAIGHT CUTS

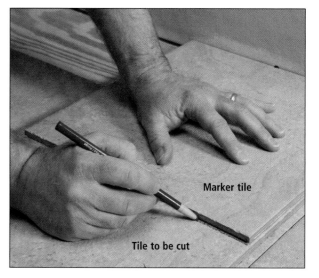

Marker tile

Tile to be cut

For a straight cut, set the tile to be cut directly on top of an installed tile. Place a marker tile over the tile to be cut, with its edge against the wall. Mark the edge with a marker. Then mark the actual cut line parallel to the edge but shorter by the width of two grout lines.

MARKING CORNER CUTS

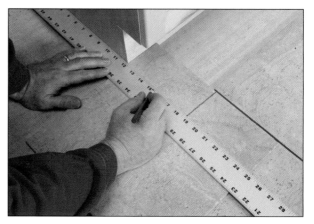

To make an L-shape cut at an outside corner, set the tile to be cut first on one side of the corner, then the other, marking the cut lines with a full tile as you would for a single straight cut. Cut each side shorter than the mark by the width of two grout lines.

MARKING CURVED CUTS

To mark a tile for a curved cut, set the tile to be cut against the pipe, lining up its edges with an installed tile. Mark the width of the cut by placing a tape measure on each side of the pipe. Reposition the tape measure to mark the depth of the cut (also see *opposite page*).

MAKING STRAIGHT CUTS

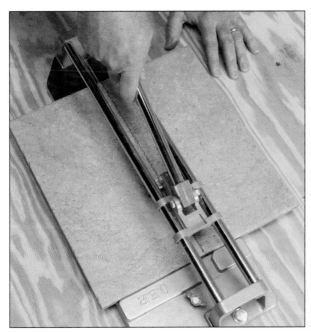

Use a snap cutter when you don't need to cut a lot of tiles. Insert the tile in the cutter, aligning the scoring wheel to the cut line. Pull or push the scoring wheel on the cut line in one pass. Hold the tile firmly with one hand and strike the handle with the heel of your other hand to snap the tile along the line.

If you have a large number of tiles to cut, rent a wet saw. Set the tile against the fence with the cut line lined up with the blade. Turn on the saw and feed the tile into the blade with light pressure. Increase the pressure as the saw cuts through the tile and ease off as the blade nears the end of the cut.

NIPPING OUT CURVED CUTS

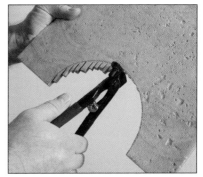

1 Use a wet saw to make several relief cuts from the edge of the tile to the curved cut line. Relief cuts do not have to be exactly parallel to each other, but make sure they stop just short of the curved line.

2 Clamp the jaws of tile nippers about an inch away from the curved line and snap out the waste.

3 Grasp the tile tightly with the tool and use a prying motion. Nip off the remaining waste a little at a time until the cut matches the curved line.

GROUTING CERAMIC TILE

Grouting starts out messy and ends up lending distinction and definition to your tile design. In fact, selecting the right grout in the right color is as important to the design of your room as selecting the tile itself. You can choose complementary grout colors or contrasting hues.

Grouting isn't difficult, but you should set aside plenty of time. It requires a sense of timing–knowing when the grout is ready for cleaning, for example. You'll develop that skill quickly. Work carefully because each step in grouting affects both the final appearance of your tiling project and its durability.

Start by acclimating the materials to the room–bring them in at least a day ahead of your grouting schedule. The temperature should be between 65 and 75 degrees.

Mix the grout by adding dry mix to the water a little at a time in a clean container–a plastic dishpan will make it easy to mix and remove with a margin trowel. Let it stand for 10 minutes and stir it again to loosen its texture. Grout should be wet, but not runny.

Lightly mist the edges of nonvitreous tile with water so they won't soak up too much moisture from the grout. Vitreous tiles do not require misting.

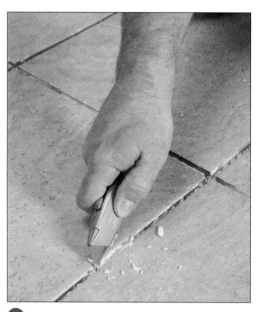

1 When the mortar dries, remove all the tile spacers before grouting, even if the manufacturer's instructions say you can grout over them. Spacers can show through the grout. Scrape any remaining mortar from the joints with a grout knife.

2 Mix up enough grout to cover about 10 square feet of tile. Pour out a small pile and pack the grout into the joints with a grout float. Hold the float at about a 30- to 45-degree angle—a sharper angle will pull the grout from the joints.

3 Working in sections, hold the float almost perpendicular to the tile and scrape off the excess. Work the float across the joints diagonally to avoid pulling up the grout. If you remove any grout, replace it and clean the surface again.

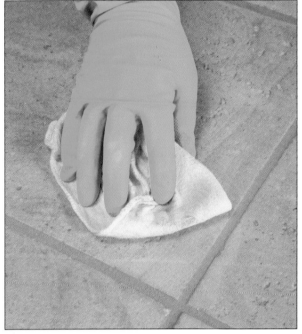

4 Let the grout set up until a just-damp sponge won't lift it from the joint. Then rub a damp sponge on the surface in a circular motion. Rinse and wring out the sponge often.

5 After about 15 minutes, remove the grout haze with a dry, clean rag. If your tile has a matte finish, you may have to clean it again with fresh water and a clean sponge.

SEALING GROUT AND TILES

CAULKING THE JOINTS

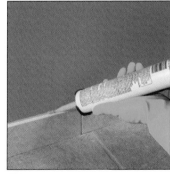

Sealing grout lines is the best way to prevent them from staining. On glazed and other impervious tiles, use an applicator designed for sealing joints. For soft-bodied tiles like saltillo, seal the entire surface using a mop or the applicator recommended by the manufacturer. Be careful when sealing stone; experiment with scrap or extra stone. Some sealers can leave stone in its natural color and others will enhance its richness.

1 Cut the nozzle of the caulking tube at a 45-degree angle and at the same width as the joint. If you're using a caulking gun, load the tube in the gun.

2 Starting in one corner, squeeze the tube or the handle of a caulk gun gently and apply the caulk to the joint. Keep the caulk gun moving so the bead won't overrun the joint. Smooth the bead with a wet finger or sponge.

GLOSSARY

Actual dimension: The actual size of a tile.

Back-butter: To apply adhesive to the back of a tile.

Backerboard: Any of several cement- or gypsum-based sheets used as substrate for setting tile.

Beater block: Manufactured or homemade tool with soft surface, often carpet. Used to set tiles level on surface.

Bisque: The clay mix that makes the tile body.

Bond strength: The measure of an adhesive's ability to resist separating from the tile and the setting bed.

Bullnose tile: Tile with at least one rounded edge. Used to finish a surface.

Cement-bodied tile: Tile formed from mortar.

Ceramic tile: A tile composed of refined clay, usually mixed with additives and kiln-fired to a minimum of 1800°F. Can be glazed or unglazed.

Cleft: Describes stone paving pieces formed by splitting smaller pieces from larger rock.

Control joint: An intentional gap cut or formed in a concrete surface to control where the surface cracks.

Dot-mounted: Process by which groups of tiles are joined by plastic dots to facilitate uniform spacing.

Down angle: A trim tile with two rounded edges used to finish off an outside corner.

Extruded: Tile shaped by pressing it into or through a die.

Field tiles: Flat tiles with unrounded edges used within the edges of a tiled installation.

Gauged stone: Stone tile cut to uniform shape and dimensions.

Glaze: A hard, usually colored layer of lead silicates and other materials fired onto the surface of a tile. Used to protect and decorate the tile surface.

Greenboard: A moisture-resistant drywall product made for wet installations.

Impervious tile: Tile with a density that resists the absorption of liquids completely.

Latex-modified thinset: Thinset mixed with latex to increase flexibility, water resistance, and adhesion.

Listello: Narrow tile formed for use in borders.

Margin trowel: A narrow rectangular trowel used for mixing mortar and applying it in narrow spaces.

Masonry cement: A mixture containing portland cement and lime. Used to bind sand or other aggregates.

Mexican paver: A handmade tile, generally low-fired or sun-dried and unglazed, characterized by blemishes, imperfections, and irregular edges.

Mil: A measurement of thickness equal to one one-thousandth (.001) of an inch.

Mortar: Any mixture of masonry cement, sand, water, and other additives.

Mosaic tile: Any tile less than 2 inches wide.

Mud: Trade jargon for cement-based mortars.

Nominal dimension: The stated size of a tile including the width of its normal grout joint.

Nonvitreous tile: Low-density tile with pores that absorb liquids readily.

Open time: The amount of time a mixed mortar can be used before it starts to set up.

Organic mastic: One of several petroleum- or latex-base adhesives.

Paver: An unglazed clay, shale, porcelain, or cement-body floor tile, ½ to 2 inches thick.

Permeability: A measure of the ability of a substance to absorb moisture.

Polymer-modified: A grout or mortar to which an acrylic or latex solution has been added.

Quarry tile: Unglazed, vitreous or semivitreous tiles, usually ¼ to ½ inch thick.

Radius trim: A trim tile whose edge turns down to form a smooth, glazed border.

Ridge-backed tile: Tile with ridges on the back, made to increase the strength of the adhesive bond.

Rod saw: A tungsten-carbide blade with a rounded surface set in a standard hacksaw frame and used for cutting curves in tile.

Saltillo tile: A soft handmade tile dried in the sun instead of being fired.

Sanded grout: Grout containing sand– increases the strength and decreases the contraction of the joint.

Semivitreous tile: Moderate-density tile that exhibits only a partial resistance to absorption of water and other liquids.

Slake: To allow a masonry mixture time after initial mixing to thoroughly absorb its liquid.

Substrate: Any of several layers, including the subfloor, beneath a tile surface.

Terra-cotta: A low-density tile made of unrefined natural clay and fired at low temperatures.

Terrazzo: Small pieces of granite or marble set in mortar often in a pattern, then polished.

Thinset mortar: Generic term used to describe a wide range of mortar-based tile adhesives.

Trim tile: Tiles with at least one rounded edge or other design for a specialized function.

Up angle: A trim tile with one rounded edge used to finish an inside corner.

V-cap: V-shape trim, often with a rounded upper corner, used to edge countertops.

Vitreous tile: An extremely dense ceramic tile with a high resistance to water absorption. Used indoors or outdoors, in wet or dry locations.

Waterproofing membrane: Any of several synthetic sheet materials used with or without adhesives to make a surface waterproof. Polyethylene and 15-pound felt paper are common examples.

INDEX